Congressional
Research
Service

Environmental Protection Agency (EPA): Appropriations for FY2013

Robert Esworthy, Coordinator
Specialist in Environmental Policy

David M. Bearden
Specialist in Environmental Policy

Mary Tiemann
Specialist in Environmental Policy

Claudia Copeland
Specialist in Resources and Environmental Policy

James E. McCarthy
Specialist in Environmental Policy

Jane A. Leggett
Specialist in Energy and Environmental Policy

September 6, 2012

Congressional Research Service

7-5700

www.crs.gov

R42520

CRS Report for Congress ————————————————————
Prepared for Members and Committees of Congress

Summary

As reported July 10, 2012, by the House Committee on Appropriations, Title II of H.R. 6091, the Interior, Environment, and Related Agencies Act, 2013, included a total of $7.06 billion for the Environmental Protection Agency (EPA) for FY2013, $1.28 billion (15.5%) below the President's FY2013 request of $8.34 billion, and $1.39 billion (16.5%) below the FY2012 enacted appropriation of $8.45 billion. Although the House committee-reported bill proposed an overall decrease for EPA, it included both decreases and increases in funding for many individual programs and activities in the eight appropriations accounts that fund the agency compared with the FY2013 requested and FY2012 enacted levels. Since FY2006, Congress has funded EPA accounts within the Interior, Environment, and Related Agencies appropriations.

The House committee-reported bill would decrease funding for seven of the eight EPA appropriations accounts compared to the President's FY2013 request, and for six of the accounts relative to FY2012 enacted levels. The largest decrease in H.R. 2061 as reported was for the State and Tribal Assistance Grants (STAG) account: $2.60 billion for FY2013, compared to $3.36 billion requested (23% decrease) and $3.61 billion for FY2012 (28% decrease). This account consistently contains the largest portion of the agency's funding among the eight accounts. The majority of the proposed decrease is attributed to a combined $507.0 million reduction in funding for grants that provide financial assistance to states to help capitalize Clean Water and Drinking Water State Revolving Funds (SRFs). Respectively, these funds finance local wastewater and drinking water infrastructure projects. H.R. 6091 as reported included $689.0 million for Clean Water SRF capitalization grants and $829.0 million for Drinking Water SRF capitalization grants, compared to $1.18 billion and $850.0 million requested for FY2013, and $1.47 billion and $917.9 million appropriated for FY2012, respectively.

The STAG account also includes funds to support "categorical" grant programs. States and tribes use these grants to support the day-to-day implementation of environmental laws, such as monitoring, permitting and standard setting, training, and other pollution control and prevention activities, and these grants also assist multimedia projects. The $994.0 million total included for FY2013 for categorical grants in H.R. 6091 as reported is $208.4 million less than the $1.20 billion requested for FY2013, and $94.8 million below the $1.09 billion FY2012 enacted amount.

Other prominent issues that have received attention within the context of EPA appropriations include the level of funding for implementing certain air pollution control requirements including greenhouse gas emission regulations, climate change research and related activities, cleanup of hazardous waste sites under the Superfund program, cleanup of sites that tend to be less hazardous (referred to as brownfields), and cleanup of petroleum from leaking underground tanks. Funding needs for the Great Lakes Restoration Initiative, and for the protection and restoration of the Chesapeake Bay and other geographic-specific water programs, also have received attention.

In addition to funding priorities among the many pollution control programs and activities, several recent and pending EPA regulatory actions continue to be controversial in the FY2013 appropriations. H.R. 6091 as reported included a number of provisions similar to those considered in the FY2012 appropriations debate (some of which were adopted for FY2012) that would restrict the use of funding for the development, implementation, and enforcement of certain regulatory actions that cut across the various pollution control statutes' programs and initiatives.

Contents

Figures

Tables

Appendixes

Contacts

Introduction

The House Committee on Appropriations reported the Interior, Environment, and Related Agencies Act, 2013, (H.R. 6091, H.Rept. 112-589), on July 10, 2012. Title II of the House committee-reported bill included a total of $7.06 billion for the Environmental Protection Agency (EPA) for FY2013, $1.29 billion (15.5%) less than the President's FY2013 request of $8.34 billion, and $1.39 billion (16.5%) less than the $8.45 billion (including applicable rescissions[1]) enacted by Congress in the Consolidated Appropriations Act, 2012 (P.L. 112-74). The Senate committee has not yet introduced a bill.

Established in 1970 to consolidate federal pollution control responsibilities that had been divided among several federal agencies, EPA's responsibilities grew significantly as Congress enacted and later amended an increasing number of environmental laws as well as major amendments to these statutes. EPA's appropriations support the agency's primary responsibilities including the regulation of air quality, water quality, pesticides, and toxic substances; the management and disposal of solid and hazardous wastes; and the cleanup of environmental contamination. EPA also awards grants to assist states and local governments in complying with federal requirements to control pollution, and to help fund the implementation and enforcement of federal regulations delegated to the states. The adequacy of federal funds to assist states with these responsibilities has become a more contentious issue over time, as state revenues and spending generally have declined under recent economic conditions.

Since FY2006, Congress has funded EPA programs and activities within the Interior, Environment, and Related Agencies appropriations bill.[2] In the annual budget resolution that is intended to guide the annual appropriations process, EPA is included within Budget Function 300 for Natural Resources and Environment, along with the Department of the Interior and other agencies. The budget resolution establishes policies and assumptions for spending and revenue for each of the federal budget functions, but the discretionary funding made available to an agency for obligation is determined in the annual appropriations process itself.[3]

The statutory authorization of appropriations for many of the programs and activities administered by EPA has expired, but Congress has continued to fund them through the appropriations process. Although House and Senate rules generally do not allow the appropriation of funding that has not been authorized, these rules are subject to points of order and are not self-enforcing. Congress may appropriate funding for a program or activity for which the authorization of appropriations has expired, if no Member raises a point of order, or the rules are waived for consideration of a particular bill. Congress typically has done so to continue the

---

[1] Title IV, Division E of P.L. 112-74, Section 436(a): "Across-the-board Rescissions - There is hereby rescinded an amount equal to 0.16 percent of the budget authority provided for fiscal year 2012 for any discretionary appropriation in titles I through IV of this Act." FY2012 enacted amounts presented in EPA's FY2013 Congressional Budget Justification include the subsequent application of the rescission. The total FY2012 enacted appropriations for the EPA in P.L. 112-74 was $8.46 billion prior to the across-the-board rescission.

[2] During the 109th Congress, EPA's funding was moved from the jurisdiction of the House and Senate Appropriations Subcommittees on Veterans Affairs, Housing and Urban Development, and Independent Agencies to the Interior, Environment, and Related Agencies Appropriations Subcommittees beginning with the FY2006 appropriations. This change resulted from the abolition of the House and Senate Appropriations Subcommittees on Veterans Affairs, Housing and Urban Development, and Independent Agencies.

[3] For information on the FY2013 budget resolution, see CRS Report R42362, *The Federal Budget: Issues for FY2013 and Beyond*, by Mindy R. Levit.

appropriation of funding for EPA programs and activities for which the authorization of appropriations has expired, but has also not funded others.[4] For FY2013 for example, the House committee exercised its option to limit funding for unauthorized programs by decreasing or terminating appropriations within the reported bill, including EPA's U.S. Mexico border grant and environmental education grant programs.[5]

In comparison to historical funding levels adjusted for inflation, the total appropriation in H.R. 2061 as reported for EPA is less than appropriations enacted by Congress in most prior fiscal years since the agency was established in FY1970 (see **Appendix A**). EPA's funding over the long term generally has reflected an increase in overall appropriations to fulfill a rising number of statutory responsibilities. Without adjusting for inflation, appropriations enacted for EPA have risen from about $1.0 billion when the agency was established in FY1970 to a peak of $14.86 billion in FY2009. The funding level that year included both the $7.64 billion in "regular" fiscal year appropriations provided in the Omnibus Appropriations Act for FY2009 (P.L. 111-8), and the $7.22 billion in emergency supplemental appropriations provided in the American Recovery and Reinvestment Act of 2009 (ARRA; P.L. 111-5). **Table A-1** in **Appendix A** provides a history of enacted appropriations (not adjusted for inflation) by EPA appropriations account from FY2008 through FY2012, and includes the House committee-reported H.R. 6091 and the FY2013 President's budget request. **Figure A-1** depicts historical funding trends (adjusted for inflation) for the agency back to FY1976, and **Figure A-2** presents EPA's full-time-equivalent (FTE) employment ceiling for FY2001 through FY2013 (proposed and requested).

In general, the term *appropriations* used in this report refers to total discretionary funds made available to EPA for obligation, including regular fiscal year and emergency supplemental appropriations, as well as any rescissions, transfers, and deferrals in a particular fiscal year, but excludes permanent or mandatory appropriations that are not subject to the annual appropriations process. This latter category of funding constitutes a very small portion of EPA's annual funding. The vast majority of the agency's annual funding consists of discretionary appropriations. Since FY1996, EPA's appropriations have been requested by the Administration and appropriated by Congress within eight statutory appropriations accounts.[6] **Appendix B** briefly describes the scope and purpose of the activities funded within each of these accounts.

In this report, the House Committee on Appropriations is the primary source for the FY2011 and FY2012 enacted amounts after rescissions,[7] and the FY2013 amounts proposed by the committee and in the President's budget request for FY2013 unless otherwise specified. Additional information regarding the FY2013 request was obtained from the EPA's *FY2013 Justification of*

---

[4] As amended, Section 202(e)(3) of the Congressional Budget and Impoundment Control Act of 1974 requires the Congressional Budget Office (CBO) to report to Congress annually on the enacted appropriations for individual programs and activities for which the authorization of appropriations has expired, and individual programs and activities for which the authorization of appropriations is set to expire in the current fiscal year. The most recent version of this report is available on CBO's website at http://www.cbo.gov/publication/42858.

[5] In its report accompanying the proposed FY2013 appropriations, the House committee concluded that no less than 51 agencies and/or programs, comprising nearly $6.0 billion in the FY2013 appropriations in the reported bill under the Interior, Environment, and Related Agencies Subcommittee's jurisdiction, are "unauthorized" or congressional authorization of appropriation has expired (H.Rept. 112-589, pp. 7-8 and pp. 136-137).

[6] Prior to FY1996, Congress appropriated funding for EPA under a different account structure, making it difficult to compare past funding levels by account over the history of the agency.

[7] The FY2011 enacted amounts reflect the application of a 0.2% across-the-board rescission included in P.L. 112-10. The FY2012 enacted amounts reflect the 0.16% across-the-board rescission included in P.L. 112-74.

Appropriation Estimates for the Committee on Appropriations (referred to throughout this report as the EPA FY2013 Congressional Justification),[8] and the President's *Budget of the United States Government, Fiscal Year 2013*, issued by the Office of Management and Budget (OMB).[9] FY2010 enacted appropriations are from the conference report to accompany the Interior, Environment, and Related Agencies Appropriations Act for FY2010 (H.R. 2996, H.Rept. 111-316, pp. 240–244). With the exception of the historical funding presented in **Figure A-1** in **Appendix A**, the enacted appropriations for prior fiscal years presented throughout this report have not been adjusted for inflation. In some cases, small increases above the prior-year funding level may reflect a decrease in real dollar values when adjusted for inflation.

Funding increases and decreases discussed in more detail in this report generally are calculated based on comparisons between the proposed funding levels reported by the House Appropriations Committee and requested by the President for FY2013, and the enacted FY2012 appropriations. This report also includes references to funding levels enacted for FY2009 for certain EPA programs and activities, including both the regular fiscal year appropriations provided in P.L. 111-8 and the emergency supplemental appropriations provided in P.L. 111-5, the latter of which is referred to throughout this report as ARRA or Recovery Act funding.

The following sections of this report provide a brief overview of FY2013 funding for EPA as proposed in the House committee-reported bill and contained the President's FY2013 budget request and enacted FY2012 for EPA. The report examines funding levels and relevant issues for selected EPA programs and activities that have received prominent attention. Appropriations are complex, and accordingly not all issues are summarized in this report.[10] Further, the appropriations bills and accompanying committee reports[11] identify funding levels for numerous programs, activities, and subactivities that are beyond the scope of this report.

EPA's FY2013 Appropriations

Table 1 presents the FY2013 amounts for EPA proposed by the House Appropriations Committee compared to the President's FY2013 budget request, and the FY2012, FY2011, and FY2010 enacted amounts by each of the agency's eight accounts (see detailed descriptions of the appropriations accounts in **Appendix B**). The enacted amounts presented in the table reflect rescissions and supplemental appropriations, where relevant. The table identifies transfers[12] of funds between the appropriations accounts, and funding levels for several program areas within certain accounts that have received prominent attention. **Figure 1** following **Table 1** presents a comparison of the allocation of the total FY2013 appropriations among the agency's eight appropriations accounts as proposed in the House committee-reported bill and the President's budget request.

---

[8] EPA's *FY2013 Justification of Appropriation Estimates for the Committee on Appropriations*, and other related agency budget documents are available at http://www.epa.gov/ocfo/budget.

[9] The multi-volume set of the President's *Budget of the United States Government, Fiscal Year 2013*, is available at http://www.whitehouse.gov/omb/budget/Overview/.

[10] OMB's document for the entire federal budget totals more than 2,000 pages, and EPA's budget justification more than 1,400, and both present an array of funding and programmatic proposals for congressional consideration.

[11] The committee reports also generally provide specific direction to the agency in terms of how the funds are to be spent to implement a certain activity.

[12] Although H.R. 6091, as reported by the House Appropriations Committee, did not include explicit statutory authority (continued...)

H.R. 6091 as reported included $7.06 billion for EPA for FY2013, 15.5% below the President's FY2013 request of $8.34 billion, and 16.5% below the FY2012 enacted appropriation of $8.45 billion provided in the Consolidated Appropriations Act, 2012 (P.L. 112-74). As indicated in **Table 1**, the overall total decrease proposed in the House committee-reported bill for EPA below the President's FY2013 request and FY2012 enacted level results largely from the proposed reductions of $753.7 million (22.5%) and $1.01 billion (28.0%), respectively, for the State and Tribal Assistance Grants (STAG) account. Most of the proposed decrease in the STAG account is attributed to a combined $507.0 million reduction below the FY2013 request and $866.3 million below FY2012 enacted funding for grants to help capitalize Clean Water and Drinking Water State Revolving Funds (SRFs) (see "Wastewater and Drinking Water Infrastructure" below).

Relative to the FY2013 President's request, the House committee-reported bill included reductions for FY2013 for nearly all other state and tribal grants funded within the STAG account, including most of the "categorical grants." Categorical grants are used by states and tribes to support the day-to-day implementation of federal environmental laws, such as monitoring, permitting and standard setting, training, enforcement, and other pollution control and prevention activities. These grants also assist multimedia projects. House committee-proposed reductions generally would fund these grants at FY2012 levels, with the exception of reductions for a subset of certain grants below the FY2012 enacted level, and an increase above FY2012 for one grant program to support wetlands development (see "Other STAG Grants" below).

Funding in House committee-reported H.R. 6091 for the remaining EPA accounts, with the exception of the Leaking Underground Storage Tank Trust Fund (LUST) account, would be below the FY2013 request. The FY2013 levels proposed in the House committee-reported bill would be below the FY2012 enacted levels for each of EPA's accounts, except for the Office of Inspector General and Buildings and Facilities accounts, which would be the same as the FY2012 enacted amounts. The House committee-reported bill included a variety of decreases and increases in funding for many of the individual programs and activities funded within the eight appropriations accounts compared to the FY2013 requested and FY2012 enacted levels.

In addition to the funding amounts presented by account in **Table 1**, the "Administrative Provisions" for EPA in Title II of H.R. 6091, as reported, included a rescission of $130.0 million from unobligated balances funded through the STAG account. The FY2012 request proposed a $30.0 million rescission of prior years' unobligated balances, but did not specify from which account. Similar rescissions of unobligated balances have been included in EPA appropriations since FY2006. For FY2012, Title II of Division E under P.L. 112-74 included a rescission of $50.0 million from unobligated balances funded through the Hazardous Substance Superfund ($5.0 million) and STAG ($45.0 million) accounts.

(...continued)

within the Superfund account to transfer funds to the Science and Technology account and the Office of Inspector General account, the committee's report on the bill did recommend funding within the Superfund account for the activities that had been supported by these transfers in past years (Research, and Audits, Evaluations, and Investigations). In its report, the committee continued to present these amounts as transfers, which would appear to presume that EPA would have some other authority to execute the transfers, as transfers from one account to another generally must be authorized in law (31 U.S.C. §1532).

**Table 1. Appropriations for the Environmental Protection Agency:
FY2010-FY2012 Enacted, the President's FY2013 Budget Request,
and House Committee-Reported H.R. 6091**

(millions of dollars; enacted amounts include rescissions and supplemental appropriations)

EPA Appropriation Accounts	FY2010 Enacted P.L. 111-88[a]	FY2011 Enacted P.L. 112-10	FY2012 Enacted P.L. 112-74	FY2013 Request	FY2013 House Committee H.R. 6091
Science and Technology					
—Base Appropriations	$848.1	$813.5	$793.7	$807.3	$738.4
—Transfer[b] in from Superfund	+$26.8	+$26.8	+$23.0	+$23.2	+$23.0
Science and Technology (with transfers)	$874.9	$840.3	$816.7	$830.5	$761.3
Environmental Programs and Management	$2,993.8	$2,756.5	$2,678.2	$2,817.2	$2,479.1
Office of Inspector General					
—Base Appropriations	$44.8	$44.7	$41.9	$48.3	$41.9
—Transfer[b] in from Superfund	+$10.0	+$10.0	+$9.9	+$10.9	+$9.9
Office of Inspector General (with transfers)	$54.8	$54.7	$51.8	$59.1	$51.9
Buildings and Facilities	$37.0	$36.4	$36.4	$42.0	$36.4
Hazardous Substance Superfund (before transfers)	$1,306.5	$1,280.9	$1,213.8	$1,176.4	$1,164.9
—Transfer[b] out to Office of Inspector General	-$10.0	-$10.0	-$9.9	-$10.9	-$9.9
—Transfer[b] out to Science and Technology	-$26.8	-$26.8	-$23.0	-$23.2	-$23.0
Hazardous Substance Superfund (after transfers)	$1,269.7	$1,244.2	$1,180.9	$1,142.3	$1,132.0
Leaking Underground Storage Tank Trust Fund Program	$113.1	$112.9	$104.1	$104.1	$104.1
Inland Oil Spill Program (formerly Oil Spill Response)	$18.4	$18.3	$18.2	$23.5	$18.2
State and Tribal Assistance Grants (STAG)					
—Clean Water State Revolving Fund	$2,100.0	$1,522.0	$1,466.5	$1,175.0	$689.0
—Drinking Water State Revolving Fund	$1,387.0	$963.1	$917.9	$850.0	$829.0
—Special Project Grants	$156.8	$0.0	$0.0	$0.0	$0.0
—Categorical Grants	$1,116.4	$1,104.2	$1,088.8	$1,202.4	$994.0
—Brownfields Section 104(k) Grants	$100.0	$99.8	$94.8	$93.3	$60.0
—Diesel Emission Reduction Grants	$60.0	$49.9	$30.0	$15.0	$30.0
—Other State and Tribal Assistance Grants	$50.0	$19.9	$15.0	$20.0	$0.0
State and Tribal Assistance Grants Total	$4,970.2	$3,758.9	$3,612.9	$3,355.7	$2,602.0
Rescissions of Unobligated Balances[c]	-$40.0	-$140.0	-$50.0	-$30.0	-$130.0
Total EPA Accounts	**$10,291.9**	**$8,682.1**	**$8,449.4**	**$8,344.5**	**$7,055.0**

Source: Prepared by the Congressional Research Service: FY2010 enacted appropriations are from the conference report to accompany the Interior, Environment, and Related Agencies Appropriations Act for FY2010 (H.R. 2996, H.Rept. 111-316, pp. 240–244). The FY2011 amounts are as provided to CRS by the House Appropriations Committee. FY2012 enacted amounts, the FY2013 requested, and House reported amounts are from the House Appropriations Committee Report (H.Rept. 112-589) accompanying H.R. 6091 as reported on July 10, 2012. The FY2011 and FY2012 enacted amounts reflect applicable rescissions. Numbers may not add due to rounding.

a. The amounts presented for the base appropriations for the Science and Technology (S&T) account and the EPA total include $2.0 million in supplemental appropriations for research of the potential long-term human health and environmental risks and impacts from the releases of crude oil, and the application of chemical dispersants and other mitigation measures under P.L. 111-212, Title II.

b. Although H.R. 6091, as reported by the House Appropriations Committee, did not include explicit statutory authority within the Superfund account to transfer funds to the Science and Technology account and the Office of Inspector General account, the committee's report on the bill did recommend funding within the Superfund account for the activities that had been supported by these transfers in past years (Research, and Audits, Evaluations, and Investigations). In its report, the committee continued to present these amounts as transfers, which would appear to presume that EPA would have some other authority to execute the transfers, as transfers from one account to another generally must be authorized in law (31 U.S.C. §1532).

c. The FY2010 enacted rescissions were from unobligated balances from funds appropriated in prior years across the eight accounts, and made available for expenditure in a later year. In effect, these "rescissions" increase the availability of funds for expenditure by the agency in the years in which they are applied, functioning as an offset to new appropriations by Congress. With regard to the FY2011 enacted rescissions, Sec. 1740 in Title VII of Div. B under P.L. 112-10 referred only to "unobligated balances available for 'Environmental Protection Agency, State and Tribal Assistance Grants'" [not across all accounts], and did not specify that these funds are to be rescinded from prior years. The EPA Administrator was to submit a proposed allocation of such rescinded amounts to the Committees on Appropriations of the House and the Senate. For FY2012 enacted, under the Administrative Provisions in Division E, Title II of P.L. 112-74, unobligated balances from the STAG ($45.0 million) and the Hazardous Substance Superfund ($5.0 million) accounts would be rescinded. FY2012 rescissions specified within the STAG account include $20.0 million from categorical grants, $10.0 million from the Clean Water SRF, and $5.0 million each from Brownfields grants, Diesel Emission Reduction Act grants, and Mexico Border. The rescission included for FY2013 in H.R. 6091 and the President's FY2013 request would be from prior years' unobligated balances within the STAG account.

**Figure 1. EPA FY2013 Appropriations Reported by Account
Requested and as Proposed in H.R. 6091 as Reported July 10, 2012
(Before Transfers Between Accounts)**

(dollars in millions)

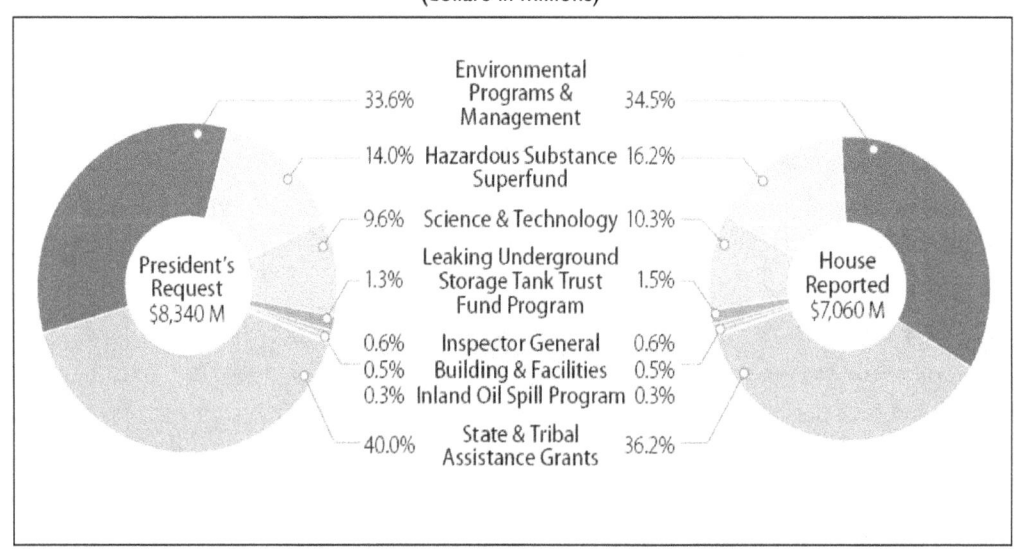

Source: Prepared by the Congressional Research Service with data from H.R. 6091 as reported by the House Committee on Appropriations and the accompanying report, H.Rept. 112-589, table pp. 170-177. Numbers may not add due to rounding.

Key Funding Issues

Much of the attention on EPA's appropriations for FY2013 has focused on federal financial assistance for wastewater and drinking water infrastructure projects,[13] various categorical grants to states to support general implementation and enforcement of federal environmental laws, funding for implementation and research support for air pollution control requirements, climate change and greenhouse gas emissions, and funding for environmental cleanup. Also garnering Congressional interest are the proposed funding levels for several geographic-specific initiatives, including the Great Lakes Restoration Initiative,[14] efforts to restore the Chesapeake Bay, and congressionally designated "National Priorities" and certain other program activities.

In commenting on the proposed reductions for EPA in its report on H.R. 6091, the House Appropriations Committee noted that EPA "continues to play an important role in protecting public and environmental health," but expressed its concern about "the efforts of EPA to expand its regulatory authority beyond what Congress intended by legislating via regulation."[15] The committee stated its position that the proposed reductions in funding would "restore a needed balance to the EPA's budget, in light of previous increases and the severe fiscal challenges facing our country." In contrast, the Minority Views included in the committee's report expressed the concern of some Members that the reductions for EPA "would put at risk the very health and safety of Americans."[16] These Members noted particular concerns about the proposed reductions in funding for EPA programs that support local drinking water and wastewater infrastructure projects, other water quality activities, science and technology to support EPA's pollution control responsibilities, and the cleanup of Superfund sites.

In addition to funding priorities among the various EPA programs and activities, several recent and pending EPA regulatory actions[17] that were central to debates on EPA's FY2011 and FY2012 appropriations again have been prominent in the debate regarding the FY2013 appropriations.[18] EPA regulatory actions issued under the Clean Air Act (CAA), in particular EPA controls on emissions of greenhouse gases, as well as efforts to address conventional pollutants, received much of the attention during the FY2012 appropriations debate and again in the FY2013 debate. Several regulatory actions under other pollution control statutes administered by EPA also have received attention. Some Members have expressed concerns related to these actions during hearings and markup of EPA's FY2013, FY2012, and FY2011 appropriations,[19] and authorizing committees continue to address EPA regulatory actions through hearings and legislation during the 112th Congress.

---

[13] See CRS Report 96-647, *Water Infrastructure Financing: History of EPA Appropriations*, by Claudia Copeland.

[14] Introduced in the FY2010 Interior Appropriations (P.L. 111-88).

[15] H.Rept. 112-589, p. 5.

[16] Ibid., p. 196.

[17] See CRS Report R41561, *EPA Regulations: Too Much, Too Little, or On Track?*, by James E. McCarthy and Claudia Copeland, for a discussion of selected EPA regulatory actions.

[18] See hearings on EPA FY2013 budget request.

[19] See CRS Report R41979, *Environmental Protection Agency (EPA) FY2012 Appropriations: Overview of Provisions in H.R. 2584 as Reported*, by Robert Esworthy. For an overview of proposed provisions contained in House-passed H.R. 1 and S.Amdt. 149, see CRS Report R41698, *H.R. 1 Full-Year FY2011 Continuing Resolution: Overview of Environmental Protection Agency (EPA) Provisions*, by Robert Esworthy.

The following sections discuss EPA issues that have generally received prominent attention in the congressional appropriations debate.

EPA Regulatory Actions

A number of administrative and general provisions in H.R. 6091 as reported July 10, 2012, address several EPA regulatory activities that were the focus of considerable debate during deliberation on EPA's FY2013 appropriations. As mentioned previously, recent actions issued related to the CAA, in particular EPA controls on emissions of greenhouse gases and efforts to address conventional pollutants (e.g., mercury, particulate matter, sulfur dioxide), received much of the attention. Several actions under the Clean Water Act, Safe Drinking Water Act, Federal Insecticide, Fungicide, and Rodenticide Act (FIFRA), and the Toxic Substances Control Act (TSCA) also received some attention. Concerns regarding these EPA actions, as well as other agencies funded in the bill, are addressed primarily in the "General Provisions." **Table C-1** through **Table C-6** in **Appendix C** present the text of those general provisions included in Title IV of H.R. 6091 impacting EPA, and include information regarding the associated sections of the bill and whether a provision was an amendment adopted during full-committee markup, if applicable.

During the past two years, EPA has proposed and promulgated a number of regulations implementing provisions of many of the federal pollution control statutes enacted by Congress. Beginning in the first session of the 112th Congress and continuing into the second session, many stakeholders and some Members have expressed concerns that the agency has been "overreaching" the authority given it by Congress, and ignoring or underestimating the costs and economic impacts of proposed and promulgated rules, and potentially overstating the associated benefits. EPA and others have countered that these actions were consistent with statutory mandates and in some cases compelled by court ruling, that the pace in many ways is slower than a decade ago, and that the costs and benefits are appropriately evaluated.[20]

The general provisions included in the House committee-reported bill would impact ongoing and anticipated EPA activities, including those addressing greenhouse gas emissions, hazardous air pollutants (e.g., asbestos), permitting of new source air emissions, water quality impacts, lead-based paint removal, environmental impacts associated with livestock operations, financial responsibility for Superfund cleanup, and stormwater discharge. Provisions include restrictions or limitations on the use of funds, and prohibitions on certain actions (e.g., permitting), as well as requirements to conduct analyses and/or report on certain activities including funding. Several of the provisions included for FY2013 in the House committee-reported bill are similar to those enacted for FY2012 (P.L. 112-74), and to a subset of those included in the House Appropriations Committee-proposed version of the FY2012 Interior, Environment, and Related Agencies Appropriations bill (H.R. 2584). P.L. 112-74 included a subset of the House-proposed provisions.[21]

---

[20] CRS Report R41561, *EPA Regulations: Too Much, Too Little, or On Track?*, by James E. McCarthy and Claudia Copeland, examines major or controversial regulatory actions taken by or under development at EPA since January 2009, providing details on the regulatory action itself, presenting an estimated timeline for completion of the rule (including identification of related court or statutory deadlines where known), and, in general, providing EPA's estimates of costs and benefits, when available. The report also discusses factors that affect the time frame in which regulations take effect.

[21] H.R. 2584 (H.Rept. 112-151) as reported by the House Appropriations Committee on July 19, 2011, and among (continued...)

Administrative Provisions

EPA "Administrative Provisions" setting terms and conditions for the use of FY2013 appropriations under Title II in H.R. 6091, as reported, contained six provisions, including a larger rescission of unobligated balances than had been requested within the STAG account and authorization for EPA to transfer funding for the Great Lakes Restoration Imitative to other federal agencies participating in this effort (discussed later in this report). Other provisions would authorize EPA to enter into cooperative agreements with federally recognized Indian tribes or Intertribal consortia; authorize collection and obligation of pesticide registration fees under FIFRA; raise the limitation on projects for construction, alteration repair, rehabilitation, and renovations of EPA facilities to $150,000 per project within S&T, EPM, Superfund, OIG, and LUST accounts; and increase the number of appointments for the Office of Research and Development under the authority provided in 42 U.S.C. 209 from the existing maximum 30 persons to 50 persons per fiscal year.

Research Activities

In its report on H.R. 6091, the House Appropriations Committee included directive language within the S&T account regarding specific EPA scientific research activities upon which some of the agency's pollution control decisions may be based. Certain directives for FY2013 build upon those included in the conference report on the FY2012 appropriations bill (H.Rept. 112-331). For example, the House Appropriations Committee directed EPA for FY2013 to make specific refinements and modifications to the agency's policies and practices for conducting human health risk assessments under the Integrated Risk Information System (IRIS).[22] EPA uses this system to establish toxicity concentrations and risk thresholds for various chemical substances, which may inform the agency's regulatory decisions under multiple pollution control statutes.

Also within the S&T account, the committee did not provide the $4.25 million increase for hydraulic fracturing research that the President had requested, and would disallow EPA from using any of the funds that would be provided in H.R. 6091 to research environmental justice impacts related to hydraulic fracturing.[23] Although the conferees on the FY2010 appropriations bill had urged EPA to study the relationship between hydraulic fracturing and drinking water,[24] the House Appropriations Committee noted in its report on H.R. 6091 that EPA had expanded its research beyond the scope of the congressionally directed study. With respect to other research related to drinking water, the committee rejected the $2.33 million reduction that the President had requested for research of innovative technologies for small drinking water systems.[25]

(...continued)

amendments considered and submitted prior to suspension of the House floor debate on July 28, 2011. Most of the administrative provisions in the FY2012 enacted appropriations were similar to those proposed in H.R. 2584 as reported and the Senate draft for FY2012, and the general provisions were similar to or a slightly revised subset of those contained in the House committee-reported bill. Comparable general provisions were not proposed in the Senate draft.

[22] H.Rept. 112-589, p. 48-49.

[23] Ibid., p. 48.

[24] H.Rept. 111-316, p. 109.

[25] H.Rept. 112-589, p. 48.

Other Programs and Activities

In its report on H.R. 6091, the House Appropriations Committee specified no FY2013 funding within the EPM account for several activities, including the greenhouse gas New Source Performance Standards; the Community Action for Renewed Environment (CARE) program; and the Northwest Forest geographic program.[26] Also under this account, no funding would be provided for EPA "Administrator Priorities." The committee noted its concern that EPA had not yet submitted a report identifying the amount of funding that the agency had allocated for the Administrator's priorities in FY2010 and FY2011, as directed in the conference report on the FY2012 appropriations bill.[27] The committee indicated that no funding would be provided in FY2013 for these priorities because of a "lack of transparency" in the nature of these activities and the lack of "performance metrics."[28] The committee directed EPA to submit a report that identifies how FY2011 and FY2012 funding was used for the Administrator priorities.[29] The committee recommended $2.20 million for the Administrator's Immediate Office and $4.24 million for the Office of Congressional and Intergovernmental Relations, the latter of which is $4.0 million below the budget request. The committee expressed concern raised by Member offices regarding a backlog of responses to congressional letters, informal questions, and questions for the record.[30]

With respect to enforcement, the committee expressed concerns regarding aerial compliance monitoring, and directed EPA to submit a report providing certain information regarding aerial monitoring activities.[31] The committee noted that EPA and the states have used aerial monitoring for nearly a decade as a "cost-effective" enforcement tool to verify compliance with environmental laws, particularly in impaired watersheds. The committee directed EPA to include information in its report on the number of enforcement actions for which aerial monitoring was used as evidence to identify a violation, and the outcome of those actions.

Wastewater and Drinking Water Infrastructure[32]

The overall decrease for FY2013 included in H.R. 6091 as reported compared to the President's FY2013 request and FY2012 enacted appropriations is largely due to the proposed reduction in EPA's STAG account for grants to aid states in capitalizing their Clean Water and Drinking Water State Revolving Funds (SRFs).[33] Historically, these grants have represented a relatively significant proportion of EPA's total appropriations. The amount approved by the House Appropriations Committee for these SRF capitalization grants represented roughly 21% of the total EPA appropriation included in H.R. 6091 as reported for FY2013. Funding for SRF grants

---

[26] Ibid., p. 51-52.

[27] H.Rept. 112-331, pp. 1075-1076.

[28] H.Rept. 112-589, p. 54.

[29] Ibid., p. 54.

[30] Ibid., p. 53.

[31] Ibid., p. 54-55.

[32] Claudia Copeland, Specialist in Resources and Environmental Policy, CRS Resources, Science, and Industry Division, was a primary contributor to this section.

[33] The STAG account also funds state and tribal "categorical" grants to support the day-to-day implementation of environmental laws. H.R. 6091 included $994.0 million to support these grant programs within the STAG account, $208.4 million less than the President's FY2013 request of $1.20 billion, and $94.8 million less than the FY2012 appropriation of $1.09 billion.

included in the President's FY2013 budget request was about 24% of the proposed total EPA funding. In FY2011 and FY2012, more than 28% of EPA's annual appropriations had been for these SRF grants within the STAG account.

As indicated in **Table 2** below, the House committee-approved $1.52 billion combined for the Clean Water and the Drinking Water SRFs for FY2013 was $507.0 million (25%) less than the $2.03 billion in the President's FY2013 request and $866.3 million (34%) less than the $2.38 billion enacted for FY2012. The combined amount was also less than the FY2011 and FY2010 enacted levels, as indicated in **Table 2**.[34] The SRF funding supports local wastewater and drinking water infrastructure projects, such as construction of and modifications to municipal sewage treatment plants and drinking water treatment plants, to facilitate compliance with the Clean Water Act and the Safe Drinking Water Act,[35] respectively.[36] EPA awards SRF capitalization grants to states and territories based on formulas.[37]

H.R. 6091 as reported included $689.0 million for the Clean Water SRF capitalization grants for FY2013, 41% below the President's FY2013 request of $1.18 billion and 53% below the FY2012 enacted level of $1.47 billion. The $829.0 million for the Drinking Water SRF capitalization grants in the House committee-reported bill was also less than the FY2013 requested and FY2012 enacted levels, but the magnitude of decrease was significantly smaller, as shown in **Table 2**.

Although the House Appropriations Committee expressed its recognition of the importance of the Clean Water and Safe Drinking Water SRFs to the states, it noted that these accounts received a combined additional $6.00 billion in the American Recovery and Reinvestment Act of 2009 (ARRA; P.L. 111-5),[38] and a "130 percent increase" in funding above FY2008 and FY2009 regular enacted appropriations in FY2010 or "... the equivalent of six years' worth of appropriations in one calendar year."[39] The House committee further asserted that funding these accounts through regular appropriations is unsustainable and must shrink under the current allocation, and encouraged the appropriate authorizing committees to examine funding mechanisms for the SRFs that are sustainable in the long term.[40] FY2013 funding levels included

---

[34] By comparison, the average annual total funding for the two SRF programs during the 12-year period prior to FY2009 was $2.0 billion.

[35] Although all of the infrastructure projects in the drinking water needs assessment would promote the health objectives of the act, EPA reported that 16% ($52.0 billion) of the funding needed was attributable to SDWA regulations, while $282.8 billion (84%) represented nonregulatory costs. Most nonregulatory funding needs typically involve installing, upgrading, or replacing transmission and distribution infrastructure to allow a system to continue to deliver safe drinking water. These system problems often do not cause a violation of a drinking water standard, but projects to correct infrastructure problems may be eligible for DWSRF funding if needed to address public health risks. Projects attributable to SDWA regulations typically involve the upgrade, replacement, or installation of treatment technologies.

[36] See CRS Report 96-647, *Water Infrastructure Financing: History of EPA Appropriations*, by Claudia Copeland, and CRS Report RS22037, *Drinking Water State Revolving Fund (DWSRF): Program Overview and Issues*, by Mary Tiemann.

[37] Clean Water SRF capitalization grants are awarded to states according to a statutory formula established in the Clean Water Act. The Drinking Water SRF capitalization grants are awarded among the states based on a formula developed administratively by EPA, using the results of a drinking water needs survey to determine allotments among the states.

[38] P.L. 111-5, the ARRA of 2009, included $4.0 billion in supplemental funding for FY2009 for the Clean Water SRF capitalization grants and $2.0 billion for the Drinking Water SRF capitalization grants.

[39] H.Rept. 112-589, p. 6.

[40] Ibid.

---

in the House committee-reported bill for the two SRF programs are the same as the amounts appropriated in FY2008.

Some Members objected to the proposed reductions, while others note that the infusion of greater resources in recent years through FY2009 supplemental funding provided under the ARRA of 2009 (P.L. 111-5) have been instrumental in meeting many local water infrastructure needs. The FY2013 request, and enacted levels for the three most recent fiscal years were larger than the regular appropriations for FY2009 in P.L. 111-8, but much smaller than total FY2009 appropriations when including the additional $4.0 billion for the Clean Water SRF capitalization grants and $2.0 billion for the Drinking Water SRF capitalization grants in P.L. 111-5 (see **Table A-1** in **Appendix A**).

Table 2. Appropriations for Clean Water and Drinking Water State Revolving Fund (SRF) Capitalization Grants: FY2010-FY2012 Enacted, Proposed for FY2013 in the President's Budget Request and House Committee-Reported H.R. 6091

(millions of dollars)

SRF	FY2010 Enacted P.L. 111-88	FY2011 Enacted P.L. 112-10	FY2012 Enacted P.L. 112-74	FY2013 Request	FY2013 House Committee H.R. 6091
Clean Water	$2,100.0	$1,522.0	$1,466.5	$1,175.0	$689.0
Drinking Water	$1,387.0	$963.1	$917.9	$850.0	$829.0
Total SRF Appropriations	**$3,487.0**	**$2,485.1**	**$2,384.4**	**$2,025.0**	**$1,528.0**

Source: Prepared by the Congressional Research Service. FY2010 enacted appropriations are from the conference report to accompany the Interior, Environment, and Related Agencies Appropriations Act for FY2010 (H.R. 2996, H.Rept. 111-316, pp. 240–244). The FY2011 amounts are as provided to CRS by the House Appropriations Committee. FY2012 enacted amounts and the FY2013 requested and proposed by the House committee are as reported in the House Appropriations Committee Report (H.Rept. 112-589) accompanying H.R. 6091 as reported on July 10, 2012. The FY2011 and FY2012 enacted amounts reflect applicable rescissions. Numbers may not add due to rounding.

The extent of federal assistance still needed to help states maintain sufficient capital in their SRFs to finance projects has been an ongoing issue.[41] Demonstrated capital needs for water infrastructure, as identified in EPA-state surveys, continue to exceed appropriated funding. Some advocates of a prominent federal role have cited estimates of hundreds of billions of dollars in long-term needs among communities, and the expansion of federal water quality requirements over time, as reasons for maintaining or increasing the level of federal assistance. Others have called for more self-reliance among state and local governments in meeting water infrastructure needs within their respective jurisdictions, and contend that reductions in federal funding for SRFs are in keeping with the need to address the overall federal deficit and federal spending concerns.

---

[41] For example, see House Transportation and Infrastructure Committee, Water Resources and Environment Subcommittee February 28, 2012, hearing entitled "A Review of Innovative Financing Approaches for Community Water Infrastructure Projects," http://transportation.house.gov/hearings/hearingdetail.aspx?NewsID=1531, and Senate Committee on Environmental and Public Works, Subcommittee on Water and Wildlife hearing entitled, "Local Government Perspectives on Water Infrastructure" February 28, 2012 http://epw.senate.gov/public/index.cfm? FuseAction=Hearings.Hearing&Hearing_id=a1ed45a6-802a-23ad-4b60-5c9fc29a8e49.

In addition to the funding levels for the SRFs, House committee-reported H.R. 6091 did not retain a requirement within the STAG account that 20% of SRF capitalization grant assistance be used for "green" infrastructure. This requirement was initially required in the American Recovery and Reinvestment Act of 2009 (ARRA; P.L. 111-5) and retained as modified in the subsequent fiscal year appropriations. Further, H.R. 6091 would require that between 20% and 30% of the funds available to each of the SRFs be used by states to provide an additional subsidy to eligible recipients in the form of forgiveness or principal, negative interest loans or grants (or a combination of these), or to restructure debt obligations.

While the SRF monies constitute the majority of EPA grant funds within the STAG account, numerous other grants also are funded within this account.

Water Infrastructure in Geographic-Specific Areas

The President's FY2013 request included funding for Alaska Native Villages and the U.S./Mexico Border water infrastructure grants projects, but the House Appropriations Committee did not provide any funding for these projects for FY2013. Enacted appropriations for FY2011 and FY2012 (and other previous fiscal years) had included funding for these geographic-specific areas:

- the FY2013 request included $10.0 million for the construction of wastewater and drinking water facilities in Alaska Native Villages, compared to $10.0 million appropriated for FY2012, $10.0 million for FY2011, and $13.0 million for FY2010; and

- $10.0 million for wastewater infrastructure projects along the U.S./Mexico border, compared to $5.0 million appropriated for 2012, $10.0 million for FY2011, and $17.0 million for FY2010.

Other STAG Grants

Some Members and state stakeholder groups[42] have expressed concerns about the adequacy of federal grant funding to assist states in carrying out federal pollution control requirements, particularly in light of recent economic conditions and the impacts on state budgets. In addition to the Clean Water and Drinking Water SRFs, and the geographic-specific area infrastructure grants discussed above, the STAG account funds "categorical grants" to states and tribes for numerous pollution control activities, as well as separate grants for Brownfields Section 104(k) projects to assess or remediate contaminated sites, Brownfields Section 128 grants to states and tribes to implement their own cleanup programs, and diesel emissions reduction grants. Brownfields grants are discussed in the section entitled "Brownfields," and the diesel emissions reduction grants are discussed in "Air Quality and Climate Change Issues," later in this report.

---

[42] For example see the Environmental Council of States (ECOS), "The State Environmental Agencies' Statement of Need and Budget Proposal for EPA's 2013 Categorical Grants STAG Budget" (State and Tribal Assistance Grants) http://www.ecos.org/files/4482_file_ECOS_Proposal_for_EPAs_2013_STAG_Budget.pdf, and other related funding publications at http://www.ecos.org/section/states/spending; see also a March 26, 2012, ECOS Press Release: Prospects for Massive Cuts in Federal Funding Alarm State Environmental Agencies, Spring Meeting Discussions, http://www.ecos.org/section/news.

Categorical Grants

H.R. 6091 as reported by the House Appropriations committee included $994.4 million to support state and tribal "categorical" grant programs within the STAG account, $203.0 million below the President's FY2013 budget of $1.20 billion, $94.8 million less than the FY2012 appropriation of $1.09 billion. EPA categorical funds are generally distributed through multiple grants to support various activities within a particular media program (air, water, hazardous waste, etc.), and are generally used to support the day-to-day implementation of environmental laws, including a range of activities such as monitoring, permitting and standard setting, training, and other pollution control and prevention activities. These grants also assist multimedia projects such as pollution prevention incentive grants, pesticides and toxic substances enforcement, the tribal general assistance program, and environmental information.

Table 3 below provides a comparison of H.R. 6091 as reported with the President's FY2013 budget request, and the three most recent fiscal years for 20 individual categorical grant programs that generally cut across six broad categories: air and radiation, water quality, drinking water, hazardous waste, pesticides and toxic substances, and multimedia. Relative to the FY2013 President's request, the House committee-reported bill included reductions for FY2013 for nearly all of the categorical grants, with a few exceptions. House committee-proposed reductions generally reflected funding of these grants at FY2012 levels, with the exception of reductions for a subset of certain grants below the FY2012 enacted level. The House committee adopted the FY2013 request's proposal to eliminate the grants for Beach Protection, but restored grant funding for Radon to the FY2012 level of $8.0 million.

The Administration's rationale for proposing to terminate funding for the Beach Protection categorical grant for FY2013 was that non-federal agencies have the capacity to run their own programs as a result of 10 years of this federal assistance. Congress appropriated $9.9 million for this categorical grant for FY2012. The Administration proposed to eliminate the Radon categorical grant, which has provided assistance to states in developing and implementing their own programs to assess and mitigate radon risks for more than 20 years. The Administration asserted that the states had developed the technical expertise and procedures to continue these efforts without federal grant assistance.[43] Under the President's FY2013 proposal, the remaining federal role in mitigating radon risks would have focused on interagency coordination of existing federal housing programs that address these risks.

As indicated in **Table 3**, the largest reduction for categorical grants included in the House committee-reported bill compared to the FY2013 request was a $100.8 million (more than 33%) decrease below the FY2013 request (from $301.5 million to $200.7 million) for State and Local Air Quality Management grants. The House committee-proposed FY2013 level for these grants is also the largest decrease ($35.0 million, 15%) below the FY2012 enacted appropriations of $235.7 million. The increase for FY2013 included in the President's FY2013 request for the Air Quality Management grants was to be used to support: permitting sources of greenhouse gas emissions; expanded state core workload for implementing revised, more stringent Clean Air Act

---

[43] For more detailed discussion of the proposed elimination of these programs and other related terminations, reductions, see OMB's Fiscal Year 2013 Budget of the United States: Cuts, Consolidations, and Savings http://www.whitehouse.gov/sites/default/files/omb/budget/fy2013/assets/ccs.pdf. See brief overview descriptions of these and other terminations in EPA's FY2013 Congressional Justification, *Highlights of Major Budget Changes,* pp. 13-19, http://www.epa.gov/planandbudget/annualplan/fy2013.html#FY13budget.

(CAA) regulations; additional air monitors; and facilitation of states' collection and review of emission data required under the Greenhouse Gas Reporting Rule.

House committee-reported H.R. 6091 also included a $61.0 million (23%) reduction below the FY2013 request for Section 106 Water Pollution Control Grants (from $265.3 million to $204.3 million). The amount was $34.1 million (14%) less than the FY2012 enacted level of $238.4 million. The Section 106 grants support efforts to prevent and develop control measures to improve water quality and address nutrient runoff. According to the EPA FY2013 Congressional Justification, the proposed $26.9 million increase above the FY2012 levels for these grants was to provide additional resources for: addressing nutrient loads; strengthening the state, interstate and tribal base programs; addressing total maximum daily load (TMDL), monitoring, and wet weather issues; and help states improve their water quality programs relating to the management of nutrients.[44] The House Appropriations Committee omitted language included in the FY2013 request to authorize additional Section 106 grants for nutrient reductions (H.Rept. 112-589, p. 66).

The House committee also did not agree to the $28.7 million (43%) increase (from $67.6 million to $96.4 million) for the Tribal Assistance Grant Program (GAP), and proposed funding these grants at the FY2012 level. Citing the agency's commitment to tribes, the Administration's proposed increase for the Tribal GAP for FY2013 was to enhance program resources to further build tribal capacity and assist tribes in leveraging other EPA and federal funding to achieve added environmental and human health protection. Other comparisons are reflected in the table that follows.

---

[44] See brief overview descriptions of these increases provided in EPA's FY2013 Congressional Justification, *Highlights of Major Budget Changes*, p. 16, http://www.epa.gov/planandbudget/annualplan/fy2013.html#FY13budget.

Table 3. Appropriations for Categorical Grants within the State and Tribal Assistance Grants (STAG) Account: FY2010-FY2012 Enacted, Proposed for FY2013 in the President's Budget Request and House Committee-Reported H.R. 6091

(millions of dollars)

Categorical Grant Program Area	FY2010 Enacted P.L. 111-88	FY2011 Enacted P.L. 112-10	FY2012 Enacted P.L. 112-74	FY2013 Requested	FY2013 House Committee H.R. 6091
Beaches Protection	$9.9	$9.9	$9.9	$0.0	$0.0
Brownfields	$49.5	$49.3	$49.3	$47.6	$47.6
Environmental Information	$10.0	$10.0	$10.0	$15.2	$10.0
Hazardous Waste Financial Assistance	$103.3	$103.1	$103.0	$103.4	$103.0
Lead	$14.6	$14.5	$14.5	$14.9	$14.5
Local Governments Climate Change Grants	$10.0	$0.0	$0.0	$0.0	$0.0
Nonpoint Source (CWA Sec. 319)	$200.9	$175.5	$164.5	$164.8	$150.5
Pesticides Enforcement	$18.7	$18.7	$18.6	$19.1	$18.6
Pesticides Program Implementation	$13.5	$13.5	$13.1	$13.1	$13.1
Pollution Control (CWA Sec. 106)	$229.3	$238.8	$238.4	$265.3	$204.3
Monitoring Grants	*$18.5*	*$18.5*	*$18.4*	*$18.5*	*$11.3*
Other Activities	*$210.8*	*$220.4*	*$220.0*	*$246.8*	*$193.0*
Pollution Prevention	$4.9	$4.9	$4.9	$5.0	$5.0
Public Water System Supervisions (PWSS)	$105.7	$105.5	$105.3	$109.7	$105.3
Radon	$8.1	$8.1	$8.0	$0.0	$8.0
State and Local Air Quality Management	$226.6	$236.1	$235.7	$301.5	$200.7
Toxic Substances Compliance	$5.1	$5.1	$5.1	$5.2	$5.1
Tribal Air Quality Management	$13.3	$13.3	$13.3	$13.6	$13.3
Tribal General Assistance Program (GAP)	$62.9	$67.7	$67.6	$96.4	$67.6
Underground Injection Control (UIC)	$10.9	$10.9	$10.9	$11.1	$10.9
Underground Storage Tanks	$2.5	$2.5	$1.5	$1.5	$1.5
Wetlands Program Development	$16.8	$16.8	$15.1	$15.2	$15.2
Total Categorical Grants	**$1,094.9**	**$1,104.2**	**$1,088.8**	**$1,202.4**	**$994.0**

Source: Prepared by the Congressional Research Service: FY2010 enacted appropriations are from the conference report to accompany the Interior, Environment, and Related Agencies Appropriations Act for FY2010 (H.R. 2996, H.Rept. 111-316, pp. 240–244). The FY2011 amounts are as provided to CRS by the House Appropriations Committee. FY2012 enacted amounts and the FY2013 requested and proposed by the House committee are as reported in the House Appropriations Committee Report (H.Rept. 112-589) accompanying H.R. 6091 as reported on July 10, 2012. The FY2011 and FY2012 enacted amounts reflect applicable rescissions. Numbers may not add due to rounding.

Air Quality and Climate Change Issues[45]

Several EPA actions under the Clean Air Act (CAA), including those addressing greenhouse gas (GHG) emissions, hazardous air pollutants (including mercury) and particulate matter emissions, have received considerable attention, including proposed legislation, during the 112th Congress and continued to be an area of interest among some Members in the consideration of FY2013 appropriations for EPA.[46] These issues were also the subject of proposals to modify or curtail EPA actions, during the FY2011[47] and FY2012[48] appropriations debate.

In addition to funding FY2013 levels for several program activities in Title II of the House committee-reported bill and in the accompanying report (see **Table 4** below), Title IV of H.R. 6091 as reported included a number of general provisions addressing EPA's use of FY2013 funds to support the development, implementation, or enforcement of CAA regulatory actions noted above, as well as directives for conducting evaluations of certain activities and providing reports to the committee. Some of these provisions were similar to general provisions included in the FY2012 Interior appropriations law (P.L. 112-74), and a subset of those proposed during deliberations on the FY2012 and FY2011 EPA appropriations.[49] Additionally, in lieu of certain general provisions proposed for FY2013 in H.R. 6091 as reported, the report accompanying the reported bill, H.Rept. 112-589, included extensive language with regard to specific climate change and air quality regulatory actions by EPA.

As indicated in **Table C-1** in **Appendix C**, general provisions contained in Title IV of the House committee-reported bill would prohibit the use of FY2013 appropriations for

- issuing permits for emissions from biological processes associated with livestock (Section 420);

- requiring reporting of GHGs from manure management systems (Section 421);

- regulating GHGs from new motor sources (Section 444);

---

[45] James E. McCarthy, and Jane A. Leggett, Specialists in Environmental Policy, CRS Resources, Science, and Industry Division were primary contributors to this section.

[46] See CRS Report R41563, *Clean Air Issues in the 112th Congress*, by James E. McCarthy; see also CRS Report R41561, *EPA Regulations: Too Much, Too Little, or On Track?*, by James E. McCarthy and Claudia Copeland, for a discussion of selected EPA regulatory actions.

[47] House-passed appropriations legislation for FY2011 (H.R. 1) included several provisions that would have restricted or prohibited use of funds for activities related to specific EPA actions under the CAA. For a more detailed summary of these provisions contained in House-passed H.R. 1, see Table 2 in CRS Report R41698, *H.R. 1 Full-Year FY2011 Continuing Resolution: Overview of Environmental Protection Agency (EPA) Provisions*, by Robert Esworthy.

[48] Partly in response to some of the concerns raised during the debate, the FY2012 appropriations law contained general provisions addressing EPA's use of FY2012 funds to support the development, implementation, or enforcement of certain Clean Air Act regulatory actions. For a more detailed discussion see CRS Report R42332, *Environmental Protection Agency (EPA) FY2012 Appropriations*, by Robert Esworthy, and CRS Report R41979, *Environmental Protection Agency (EPA) FY2012 Appropriations: Overview of Provisions in H.R. 2584 as Reported*, by Robert Esworthy.

[49] Congress has addressed EPA's development of CAA regulations through the appropriations process in the past—either explicitly providing or restricting the availability of agency funds for such purposes—and these issues were debated extensively during the FY2012 and FY2011 appropriations process. See CRS Report R42332, *Environmental Protection Agency (EPA) FY2012 Appropriations*, by Robert Esworthy, and CRS Report R41698, *H.R. 1 Full-Year FY2011 Continuing Resolution: Overview of Environmental Protection Agency (EPA) Provisions*, by Robert Esworthy.

- administering or enforcing the National Emission Standards for Hazardous Air Pollutants regulations for asbestos for residential buildings with four or fewer units (Section 446);

- issuing or enforcing standards of performance applicable to emission of GHGs by any new or existing electric utility generating unit (Section 448).

The general provisions also included requirements for EPA to conduct a 48-month pilot project for the North American Emission Control Area (which requires the use of low sulfur fuels by ships within 200 miles of the U.S. coast) jointly with the U.S. Coast Guard (Section 440), development of a seventh edition of the document entitled "EPA Air Pollution Control Cost Manual" (Section 449), and publication in the *Federal Register* of a notice to solicit comment on revising the agency's "Guideline on Air Quality Models" (Section 405).

More broadly, in its report the House committee expressed skepticism with regard to the repackaging of existing program activities and funding new ones as "climate change programs," noting that in the Interior, Environment, and Related Agencies Appropriations alone, funding for programs identified as "climate change" nearly doubled from $192.0 million to $372.0 million between FY2008 and FY2011.[50] Citing its concern with the number of new seemingly duplicative programs and a lack of effective coordination and communication of climate change activities, budgets, and accomplishments across the federal government, the House committee proposed cutting climate change funding by 29% in H.R. 6091 as reported.[51] Similar to the FY2012 appropriations, the House committee-reported bill included a general provision in Title IV (Section 419) that would require the President to submit a comprehensive report to the House and Senate Appropriations Committees detailing all federal (including EPA) fiscal year obligations and expenditures, domestic and international, for climate change programs and activities by agency for FY2012.[52]

EPA is one of 17 federal agencies that have received appropriations for climate change activities in recent fiscal years. EPA's share of this funding is relatively small, but EPA's policy and regulatory roles are proportionately larger than other federal agencies and departments.

Appropriated funds for EPA's climate change and air quality actions are distributed across several program activities under multiple appropriations accounts. Because of variability in these activities and modifications to account structures from year to year, it is difficult to compare the overall combined funding included in appropriations bills with the President's request[53] and prior-year enacted appropriations. However, comparisons can be made among certain activities for which Congress does specify a line-item in the appropriations process. **Table 4** below presents a comparison, when possible,[54] of the House committee-reported bill for FY2013 with the

---

[50] See H.Rept. 112-589, p. 9.

[51] Ibid.

[52] The provision is similar to a reporting requirement for FY2009 and FY2010 Department of the Interior, Environment, and Related Agencies Appropriations, and to a recurring reporting requirement that had been in existence for nearly a decade through FY2007, under provisions in the annual appropriations bills for Foreign Operations.

[53] Congress does not appropriate funding based on EPA's strategic performance goals; however, the President's FY2013 request included $1.12 billion for FY2013 across multiple appropriations accounts to support the agency's strategic objective: "Taking Action on Climate Change and Improving Air Quality," $98.4 million above the FY2012 level of $1.03 billion (EPA's FY2013 Congressional Justification, pp. 15-32, http://www.epa.gov/planandbudget/ annualplan/fy2013.html#FY13budget).

[54] It is difficult to compare the FY2013 request for all program activities with previous fiscal years' appropriations, as (continued...)

President's FY2013 request and FY2010 through FY2012 enacted appropriations for air quality and climate change program activities within various EPA appropriations accounts. The program activities included in the table are as typically presented in funding tables included in EPA's congressional justifications and in congressional appropriations committee reports.

As an example, the House committee-reported bill would provide a total of $372.5 million for FY2013 within the EPM and the S&T accounts for EPA "clean air and climate" programs, compared to the President's FY2013 request of $440.2 million, and the FY2012 appropriation of $410.5 million. The House committee did not provide requested increased funding within the S&T account for implementation of the Cross-State Air Pollution Rule,[55] and provided no funding in the EPM account for greenhouse gas New Source Performance Standards.[56] Also within the S&T account, the House committee-reported bill included $95.0 million for "Research: Air, Climate, and Energy" for FY2013, compared to FY2013 requested $105.9 million, and FY2012 enacted $98.8 million.[57] Much of the increase above the FY2012 enacted level included in the President's FY2013 request is largely the result of a proposed $27.1 million (9.5%) increase above the FY2012 enacted amount of $286.1 million for Climate Change and Air Quality in the EPM account. Also as indicated in **Table 4**, the House committee-reported bill included $256.7 million for this program area. As indicated in the table, there was variability across the multiple program activities funded under S&T and EPM accounts when comparing proposed FY2013 amounts with the previous fiscal years' enacted levels.

As discussed in the previous section of this report, under the STAG account, the House committee-reported bill included $200.7 million for State and Local Air Quality Management grants, $100.8 million (33%) less than the FY2013 request of $301.5 million, and $35.0 million (15%) less than the FY2012 enacted level of $235.7 million. Within this line item, the House committee stated that no funds would be provided for greenhouse gas (GHG) permitting grants, or for the GHG reporting rule within this program activity.[58] States use these federal funds to help pay the costs of operating their air pollution control programs. Much of the day-to-day operations of these programs (i.e., monitoring, permitting, enforcement, and developing site-specific regulations) is done by the states with federal Clean Air Act authorities delegated to them by EPA. The National Association of Clean Air Agencies (NACAA) testified that the Clean Air Act (CAA) authorizes federal grants to the states for up to 60% of the costs of running these state and local air quality programs; however, NACAA noted that the grant amounts have declined over the last decade, with the federal contribution falling to roughly 25% of the total cost of these programs.[59]

(...continued)

from year to year, EPA has sometimes modified the line-items under which funding for climate protection related program activities is requested. For example, for FY2012 conferees accepted the Administration's proposed budget reorganization of certain air quality and climate protection program activities, including consolidation and modifications of various line-items, making it difficult to compare FY2012 appropriations with FY2011 (and prior year) appropriations.

[55] H.Rept. 112-589, p. 47.

[56] H.Rept. 112-589, p. 51.

[57] H.Rept. 112-589, see table on pp. 170-171.

[58] H.Rept. 112-589, p. 66.

[59] National Association of Clean Air Agencies (NACAA) Testimony Provided to the Senate Appropriations Committee Subcommittee on Interior, Environment, and Related Agencies Regarding the FY 2013 Budget for the U.S. Environmental Protection Agency, April 17, 2012, http://www.4cleanair.org/Documents/ SenateTestimonyNACAAFY2013FINAL.pdf.

According to the EPA FY2013 Congressional Justification, of the total $65.8 million requested increase for FY2013 for these air quality management categorical grants, $39.0 million would have supported the core state workload for implementing revised and more stringent federal National Ambient Air Quality Standards, including the installation of additional air quality monitors and overseeing compliance with air toxics regulations. Another $26.5 million of the increase for these grants in the STAG account was to support states and tribes in permitting sources of GHG emissions and implementing the federal GHG Reporting Rule.[60]

Also within the STAG account, the House committee included $30.0 million for the Diesel Emission Reduction Grants program for FY2013, $15.0 million more than the FY2013 request and roughly the same as FY2012. The ARRA of 2009 (P.L. 111-5) provided an additional $300.0 million in supplemental funds for these grants in FY2009 for a total of $360.0 million in FY2009, much of which was awarded in FY2010. The Energy Policy Act of 2005 (EPAct 2005)[61] authorized $200.0 million annually for these grants from FY2007 through FY2011. The House committee-reported bill also would reinstate funding for state indoor radon (categorical) grants at the FY2012 level of $8.0 million. As indicated previously, the FY2013 request proposed eliminating the Radon grant program, noting that states had established the necessary technical expertise and program funding in place to continue radon protection efforts without federal funding.[62]

Although some Members and stakeholders have raised concerns about the proposed funding for various air quality programs in the President's FY2013 budget request, much of the attention during deliberations on the FY2013 appropriations and other recent fiscal years has focused less on the adequacy of this funding and more on the costs and economic impacts of several EPA regulatory actions to address air quality and climate change. For example, although relatively minor in terms of EPA's funding, the agency's responses to a 2007 U.S. Supreme Court decision[63] remain a prominent topic of debate. This decision found greenhouse gases (GHGs) to be "air pollutants" within the Clean Air Act's definition of that term, and required EPA to consider, among other things, whether GHGs endanger public health or welfare. The EPA's "endangerment finding" was the first step in promulgating regulations to limit emissions, which led to concerns among affected stakeholders and within Congress about the potential costs of compliance and the economic impacts of such regulations.

---

[60] *EPA's FY2013 Congressional Justification*, "Taking Action on Climate Change and Improving Air Quality," pp. 15-16 (pdf pp. 23-24), http://www.epa.gov/planandbudget/annualplan/fy2013.html#FY13budget.

[61] Energy Policy Act of 2005, P.L. 109-58, Title VII, Subtitle G.

[62] An additional reduction of $1.7 million (43.6%) for other EPA radon program activities was proposed in the FY2013 request within the EPM account, from $3.9 million enacted for FY2012 to $2.2 million requested for FY2013. See references in EPA's FY2013 Congressional Justification, pp.15-16, 20-21, 777-778 (http://www.epa.gov/planandbudget/annualplan/fy2013.html#FY13budget).

[63] *Massachusetts v. EPA*, 549 U.S. 497 (2007).

Table 4. Appropriations for Selected EPA Air Quality Research and Implementation Activities by Account: FY2010-FY2012 Enacted, Proposed for FY2013 in the President's Budget Request and House Committee-Reported H.R. 6091

(millions of dollars)

Account/Program Area	FY2010 Enacted P.L. 111-88	FY2011 Enacted P.L. 112-10	FY2012 Enacted P.L. 112-74	FY2013 Requested	FY2013 House Committee H.R. 6091
Science and Technology Account					
Clean Air and Climate	—	—	$124.4	$127.1	$115.8
Clean Air Allowance Trading Program	—	—	$9.1	$9.8	—
Climate Protection Program	—	—	$16.3	$7.8	$7.8
Federal Support for Air Quality Management	—	—	$7.1	$7.6	
Federal Support for Air Toxics Program	—	—	$0.0	$0.0	—
Federal Vehicle & Fuels Standards & Certification	—	—	$91.9	$101.9	$91.9
Indoor Air and Radiation	$1.2	$1.3	$6.8	$6.7	$6.7
Indoor Air: Radon Program	—	—	$0.2	$0.0	—
Reduce Risks from Indoor Air	—	—	$0.4	$0.4	—
Radiation: Protection	—	—	$2.1	$2.1	—
Radiation: Response Preparedness	—	—	$4.1	$4.2	—
	—	—			
Research: Air, Climate and Energy	—	—	$98.8	$105.9	$95.0
Global Change	—	—	$18.3	$20.3	$15.8
Clean Air	—	—	$78.5	$82.8	$77.2
Other Activities	—	—	$2.0	$2.6	
Air Toxics and Quality	$121.9	$120.5	—	—	—
Climate Protection Program	$19.8	$16.8	—	—	—
Research: Clean Air	$102.7	$102.4	—	—	—
Research: Global Change	$20.9	—	—	—	—
Environmental Programs and Management					
Clean Air and Climate	—	—	$286.1	$313.2	$256.7
Clean Air Allowance Trading Program	—	—	$20.8	$20.9	—
Climate Protection Program:	$113.0	$107.5	$99.5	$108.0	$84.9
- Climate Protection Program: Energy STAR	$52.6	—	$49.7	$53.9	$48.1
- Climate Protection Program: Methane to Markets	$4.6	—	$5.0	$4.9	—
- Climate Protection Program: Greenhouse Gas Registry	$16.7	—	$15.8	$18.7	$6.4
- Climate Protection Program: Other Activities	$39.1	—	$29.0	$30.5	—
Federal Stationary Source Regulations	—	—	$27.3	$34.1	$20.6

Account/Program Area	FY2010 Enacted P.L. 111-88	FY2011 Enacted P.L. 112-10	FY2012 Enacted P.L. 112-74	FY2013 Requested	FY2013 House Committee H.R. 6091
Federal Support for Air Quality Management	—	—	$123.5	$134.8	$115.3
Federal Support for Air Toxics Program	—	—	$0.0	$0.0	—
Stratospheric Ozone: Domestic Programs	—	—	$5.6	$5.6	—
Stratospheric Ozone: Multilateral Fund	—	—	$9.5	$9.7	—
Indoor Air and Radiation	$26.6	$25.9	$33.7	$32.4	$32.4
Indoor Air: Radon Program	—	—	$3.9	$2.2	—
Reduce Risks from Indoor Air	—	—	$17.2	$17.4	—
Radiation: Protection	—	—	$9.6	$9.8	—
Radiation: Response Preparedness	—	—	$3.0	$3.1	—
Air Toxics and Quality	$202.2	$207.3	—	—	—
Hazardous Substance Superfund Account					
Indoor Air and Radiation: Radiation Protection	—	—	$2.5	$2.6	$2.5
Air Toxics and Quality	$2.5	$2.5	—	—	—
State and Tribal Assistance Grants Account					
Diesel Emissions Reduction Grants (Energy Policy Act)	$60.0	$49.9	$30.0	$15.0	$30.0
Local Government Climate Change Grants	$10.0	$0.0	$0.0	$0.0	—
Targeted Airshed Grants	$20.0	$0.0	—	—	—
Radon	$8.1	$8.1	$8.0	$0.0	$8.0
State & Local Air Quality Management Grants	$226.6	$236.1	$235.7	$301.5	$200.7
Tribal Air Quality Management Grants	$13.3	$13.3	$13.3	$13.6	$13.3

Source: Prepared by the Congressional Research Service: FY2010 enacted appropriations are from the conference report to accompany the Interior, Environment, and Related Agencies Appropriations Act for FY2010 (H.R. 2996, H.Rept. 111-316, pp. 240–244). The FY2011 and FY2012 enacted amounts and the FY2013 requested amounts are as provided to CRS by the House Appropriations Committee, and EPA's *"FY2013 Justification of Appropriation Estimates for the Committee on Appropriations,"* http://www.epa.gov/planandbudget/ annualplan/fy2013.html#FY13budget. FY2013 proposed by the House committee are as reported in the House Appropriations Committee report (H.Rept. 112-589) accompanying H.R. 6091 as reported on July 10, 2012. The FY2011 and FY2012 enacted amounts reflect applicable rescissions. Numbers may not add due to rounding.

Note: The "—" denoted in the table indicates that comparable data are unavailable. It is difficult to compare the FY2013 request and FY2012 enacted amounts for all program activities with previous fiscal years' appropriations because from year to year EPA has sometimes modified the line-items under which funding for climate protection related program activities is requested. For FY2012, the conferees accepted the Administration's proposed budget reorganization of certain air quality and climate protection program activities, including consolidation and modifications of various line-items, making it difficult to compare FY2012 appropriations with FY2011 (and prior year) appropriations.

Cleanup of Superfund Sites[64]

The Hazardous Substance Superfund (Superfund) account supports the assessment and cleanup of sites contaminated from the release of hazardous substances. EPA carries out these activities under the Superfund program. The Comprehensive Environmental Response, Compensation, and Liability Act of 1980 (CERCLA) authorized this program, and established the Superfund Trust Fund to finance discretionary appropriations to fund it.[65] As reported by the House Appropriations Committee, H.R. 6091 would provide a total of $1.16 billion for the Superfund account in FY2013. The committee's recommendation is $11.5 million (1%) less than the President's FY2013 request of nearly $1.18 billion, and $48.9 million (4%) less than the FY2012 enacted appropriation of $1.21 billion. These amounts reflect an overall downward funding trend since FY2010. (See **Table 5**.) For the previous decade, annual funding levels for the Superfund account had remained fairly steady, averaging approximately $1.25 billion annually.[66] However, some have observed that the funding levels declined during this period when accounting for the effects of inflation.

As amended, CERCLA authorizes EPA's Superfund program to clean up sites that are among the nation's most hazardous and to enforce the liability of parties who are responsible for the cleanup costs.[67] Many states also have developed their own cleanup programs to address contaminated sites that are not pursued at the federal level. These state programs complement federal cleanup efforts. At sites that are addressed under the federal Superfund program, EPA first attempts to identify the responsible parties to enforce their liability for the cleanup costs. Sites financed by the responsible parties do not rely upon Superfund appropriations, except for situations in which EPA may use the appropriations up front and later recover the costs from the responsible parties. If the responsible parties cannot be found or do not have the ability to pay, EPA is authorized to use Superfund appropriations to pay for the cleanup of a site under a cost-share agreement with the state in which the site is located.[68] Sites at which there are no viable parties to assume responsibility for the cleanup are referred to as "orphan" sites.

The use of Superfund appropriations has focused primarily on cleaning up contamination from the release of hazardous substances at high-risk sites that EPA has placed on the National Priorities List (NPL).[69] The cleanup of federal facilities on the NPL is funded apart from the Superfund program by the federal agencies that administer those facilities.[70] Annual funding for the cleanup of all contaminated federal facilities combined exceeds EPA's Superfund

---

[64] This section was written by David M. Bearden, Specialist in Environmental Policy, CRS Resources, Science, and Industry Division.

[65] 42 U.S.C. §9601 et seq.

[66] FY2009 was an exception to this trend, with $600.0 million in supplemental funds provided in ARRA (P.L. 111-5).

[67] For more information on EPA's cleanup and enforcement authorities under CERCLA, see CRS Report R41039, *Comprehensive Environmental Response, Compensation, and Liability Act: A Summary of Superfund Cleanup Authorities and Related Provisions of the Act*, by David M. Bearden.

[68] State cost-share requirements apply only to the performance of long-term Remedial actions, but not to short-term Removal actions to address more imminent hazards and emergency situations.

[69] For information on the number of sites that EPA has placed on the NPL over time and their listing status, see the Superfund Program website: http://www.epa.gov/superfund/sites/npl/status.htm. CERCLA also authorizes EPA to use Superfund appropriations for performing short-term Removal actions at sites not listed on the NPL.

[70] The use of cleanup appropriations at federal facilities has been limited to the performance of the cleanup itself. The Judgment Fund administered by the U.S. Treasury has been the source of monies for the payment of claims for cleanup liability that may be submitted against the United States at sites where a federal agency is a liable party.

---

appropriations by several billion dollars. Although Superfund appropriations are not eligible to pay for the cleanup of federal facilities, EPA oversees their cleanup through the Superfund program in conjunction with the states in which the facilities are located.

The Superfund account also funds EPA's homeland security responsibilities to prepare for the federal response to incidents that may involve the intentional release of hazardous substances, EPA's operational and administrative expenses in carrying out the Superfund program, and EPA's enforcement of cleanup liability under CERCLA. Enforcement is a core tenet of the statute intended to ensure that the responsible parties pay for the cleanup of contamination whenever possible, in order to focus the use of Superfund appropriations at orphan sites. Most of the decrease that the House Appropriations Committee recommended for the Superfund account in FY2013 would be for EPA's operational and administrative expenses, and the enforcement of cleanup liability. Although a decrease in the enforcement budget may yield savings in the near term, the need for appropriations possibly could rise in the future if less enforcement were to result in fewer parties contributing to cleanup costs, and more of the costs being shifted to the taxpayer. Although the committee proposed an overall decrease for the Superfund account, it recommended an increase above the President's FY2013 request for long-term Remedial actions to clean up sites on the NPL, but at a lower funding level than enacted for FY2012.

Historically, funding within the Superfund account also has been transferred to EPA's Science and Technology account for the research and development of cleanup technologies, and to EPA's Office of Inspector General account for independent auditing, evaluation, and investigation of the Superfund program. In past years, annual appropriations acts have included statutory language authorizing these transfers. The House Appropriations Committee's report on H.R. 6091 recommended funding for these activities within the Superfund account at the same level as enacted for FY2012. However, the committee did not include explicit statutory authority in the bill itself to transfer these funds to the Science and Technology account and the Office of Inspector General account, a departure from past appropriations acts. The committee continued to present the funding levels as transfers in the tables accompanying its report, which would appear to presume that EPA would execute the transfers under some other authority.[71] Generally, transfers of appropriations from one account to another must be authorized in law.[72]

Table 5 presents the House Appropriations Committee's recommended funding levels for the Superfund account in FY2013 by major program area, compared to the President's FY2013 request, and appropriations enacted from FY2010 through FY2012. Transfers to the Science and Technology account and the Office of Inspector General account are presented consistent with the committee's report on H.R. 6091.

---

[71] H.Rept. 112-589, pp. 171, 173, and 174.

[72] 31 U.S.C. §1532. For further discussion of appropriations transfer authority, see Government Accountability Office, *Principles of Federal Appropriations Law*, Third Edition, Volume I, GAO-04-261SP, January 2004, p. 2-24, available on GAO's website: http://www.gao.gov/legal/redbook/redbook.html.

Table 5. Appropriations for the Hazardous Substance Superfund Account: FY2010-FY2012 Enacted, and Proposed for FY2013 in the President's Budget Request and House Committee-Reported H.R. 6091

(millions of dollars)

Program Area and Transfers to Other EPA Accounts	FY2010 Enacted P.L. 111-88	FY2011 Enacted P.L. 112-10	FY2012 Enacted P.L. 112-74	FY2013 President's Request	FY2013 House Committee H.R. 6091
Remedial	$605.0	$605.4	$565.0	$531.8	$546.8
Emergency Response and Removal	$202.8	$200.5	$189.6	$188.5	$188.5
Federal Facilities (Oversight)	$32.2	$31.1	$26.2	$26.8	$26.2
Enforcement	$196.0	$191.6	$186.7	$184.4	$169.4
Operations and Administration	$137.9	$136.6	$135.8	$140.4	$130.8
Homeland Security	$56.6	$41.7	$41.8	$41.9	$41.9
Other Program Areas	$78.0	$74.0	$68.7	$62.6	$61.3
Total Superfund Account	**$1,308.5**	**$1,280.9**	**$1,213.8**	**$1,176.4**	**$1,164.9**
Transfer to Science and Technology	-$26.8	-$26.8	-$23.0	-$23.2	-$23.0
Transfer to Office of Inspector General	-$10.0	-$10.0	-$9.9	-$10.9	-$9.9
Superfund Account After Transfers[a]	**$1,271.7**	**$1,244.1**	**$1,180.9**	**$1,142.3**	**$1,132.0**

Source: Prepared by the Congressional Research Service. FY2010 enacted amounts are as presented in the conference report to accompany the Interior, Environment, and Related Agencies Appropriations Act for FY2010 (H.R. 2996, H.Rept. 111-316, pp. 240–244). FY2011 enacted amounts are the prior-year amounts presented by the House Appropriations Committee in its report accompanying the Interior, Environment, and Related Agencies Appropriations Bill, 2012 (H.R. 2584, H.Rept. 112-151, pp. 192-200). FY2012 enacted amounts, and the FY2013 proposed amounts, are as presented by the House Appropriations Committee in its report accompanying the Interior, Environment, and Related Agencies Appropriations Bill, 2013 (H.R. 6091, H.Rept. 112-589, pp. 170-177). FY2011 and FY2012 enacted amounts reflect applicable rescissions. Numbers may not add due to rounding.

a. Although H.R. 6091, as reported by the House Appropriations Committee, did not include explicit statutory authority within the Superfund account to transfer funds to the Science and Technology account and the Office of Inspector General account, the committee's report on the bill did recommend funding within the Superfund account for the activities that had been supported by these transfers in past years (Research, and Audits, Evaluations, and Investigations). In its report, the committee continued to present these amounts as transfers, which would appear to presume that EPA would have some other authority to execute the transfers, as transfers among accounts generally must be authorized in law (31 U.S.C. §1532).

The following sections discuss selected issues that have received more prominent attention in the appropriations and budget debate, including the adequacy of funding for long-term Remedial actions at NPL sites, overall cleanup progress, the development of Superfund financial responsibility requirements, the management of private settlement funds in Superfund Special Accounts, the use of Superfund Alternative agreements in lieu of listing sites on the NPL, and proposals to reinstate Superfund taxes to augment resources available for appropriation.

Remedial Projects

CERCLA authorizes two types of cleanup actions at individual sites. Remedial actions are intended to address long-term risks to human health and the environment, whereas Removal actions are intended to address more imminent hazards or emergency situations. In the Superfund cleanup process, Removal actions may precede Remedial actions to stabilize site conditions while

Remedial actions are developed and constructed. Only sites listed on the NPL are eligible for Superfund appropriations to pay for Remedial actions, whereas Removal actions may be funded with Superfund appropriations regardless of whether a site is listed on the NPL.[73] The pace of long-term cleanup efforts at many sites has raised concerns among Members of Congress, states, and affected communities about the adequacy of funding for Remedial projects.

The House Appropriations Committee recommended $546.8 million for Remedial projects in FY2013, an increase of $15.0 million above the President's request of $531.8 million, but $18.2 million less than the FY2012 enacted appropriation of $565.0 million. In its report on H.R. 6091, the committee stated its concern about the President's requested "deep cuts" for Remedial projects while requesting "marginal reductions or increases" for other activities funded within the Superfund account, and stated its position that the President's request reflects a "wrong distribution of funds for the Superfund account."[74] The House Appropriations Committee approved the smaller $1.1 million reduction that the President had requested for Removal projects, from $189.6 million enacted for FY2012 to $188.5 million for FY2013. The President had proposed a smaller reduction for Removal projects to focus priorities on near-term risks, as opposed to Remedial projects that address long-term risks.

EPA had acknowledged in its FY2013 Congressional Justification that the requested decrease for Remedial projects could have an impact on the pace of long-term cleanup efforts.[75] EPA had indicated that available funding would be prioritized for continuing ongoing Remedial Projects, with no new construction projects planned in FY2013. However, new Remedial projects still could begin at sites financed by the responsible parties, which do not rely on Superfund appropriations. Although EPA had cited federal budgetary constraints as a reason for the proposed decrease for Remedial projects, the agency indicated at the same time that state budgetary constraints have resulted in some sites being deferred to the federal Superfund program.[76] Federal involvement at these sites could increase demands for appropriations. EPA emphasized that it would continue its policy of enforcing the liability of responsible parties first to reserve available appropriations for orphan sites.

Cleanup Progress

The long-standing debate over the adequacy of funding for the Superfund program has centered primarily on the pace and adequacy of cleanup at NPL sites. EPA mainly has used the measure of "construction completion" to track overall cleanup progress at individual sites over the life of the program. This measure generally indicates that all long-term cleanup remedies are in place and operating as intended, after which point operation and maintenance of the remedies may continue for years, or even decades in some instances.[77] The annual number of construction completions has been declining for more than a decade, from a high of 88 in FY1997 to a low of 18 in FY2010, and increasing to 22 in FY2011.[78] EPA has estimated 22 construction completions again

---

[73] 40 C.F.R. §300.425(b).

[74] H.Rept. 112-589, p. 61.

[75] See EPA's FY2013 Congressional Justification, p. 40.

[76] See EPA's FY2013 Congressional Justification, p. 679.

[77] For information on the use of construction completion as a measure of cleanup progress at individual sites, see EPA's Superfund program website: http://www.epa.gov/superfund/cleanup/ccl.htm.

[78] The number of construction completions from FY1995 through FY2011, and so far in FY2012, is available on EPA's Superfund program website: http://www.epa.gov/superfund/sites/query/queryhtm/nplfy.htm.

in FY2012, and 19 in FY2013 based on the President's budget request. This overall downward trend since the late 1990s has raised questions as to whether annual appropriations for the Superfund program have been adequate to maintain consistent progress to ensure protection of human health and the environment. In its report on H.R. 6091, the House Appropriations Committee commented on EPA's projected reduction in the number of construction completions and other performance measures for FY2013. The committee stated its position that the slowed pace is "wrong policy for addressing the nation's most contaminated hazardous waste sites."[79] The committee cited this concern in recommending a higher level of funding for Remedial projects than the President had requested.

Although there has been much focus on the impacts of funding on the pace of cleanup, funding alone is not the sole factor that determines how quickly cleanup may proceed. The scope and complexity of cleanup challenges at individual sites, and technological capabilities, can be significant factors as well. Consequently, greater time may be required to complete construction at larger and more complex sites. Furthermore, measuring the completion of construction on a site-wide basis alone does not reflect progress made among individual projects. In some cases, the construction of nearly all of the individual projects at a site may be complete, but the site is not designated as construction complete until all projects are completed.[80]

Financial Responsibility Requirements

As reported by the House Appropriations Committee, Section 447 of H.R. 6091 would prohibit EPA from using any funds that would be provided in that bill for the agency to "develop, propose, finalize, implement, enforce, or administer" Superfund financial responsibility requirements for facilities that manage hazardous substances. Section 108(b) of CERCLA directed the President to identify the initial classes of facilities that would be subject to these requirements no later than December 11, 1983, and to promulgate the requirements *no earlier* than December 11, 1985. Section 108(b) stated that the purpose of the requirements is for facilities to "establish and maintain evidence of financial responsibility consistent with the degree and duration of risk associated with the production, transportation, treatment, storage, or disposal of hazardous substances."[81] Implementation of Section 108(b) is delegated to EPA by executive order, with the exception of transportation facilities delegated to the Department of Transportation (DOT).[82]

The lack of action by EPA and DOT in identifying classes of facilities and promulgating financial responsibility requirements for those classes was challenged by environmental groups in a citizen suit. In February 2009, the court found that the groups had shown standing to sue EPA, but not DOT, and held that under CERCLA, EPA had a non-discretionary duty to identify classes of facilities for establishing financial responsibility requirements by the act's deadline.[83] The court therefore ordered EPA to identify those classes. In August 2009, the court acknowledged that EPA had by then fulfilled its obligation to identify the initial classes of facilities (specifically hardrock mining facilities), albeit years later than the statutory deadline of December 11, 1983.[84] The court

---

[79] H.Rept. 112-589, p. 61.

[80] EPA has begun to separately track the number of Remedial projects completed at each site to reflect progress toward achieving construction completion on a site-wide basis.

[81] 42 U.S.C. §9608(b).

[82] Executive Order 12580, Superfund Implementation, January 23, 1987, 52 *Federal Register* 2923.

[83] Sierra Club v. Johnson, 2009 Westlaw 482248 (N.D. Cal. February 25, 2009).

[84] Sierra Club v. Johnson, 2009 Westlaw 2413094 (N.D. Cal. August 5, 2009).

held, however, that plaintiffs' remaining claim, seeking an order that EPA take the next step of promulgating financial responsibility requirements, had to be rejected. The absence of a statutory deadline for such promulgation, combined with legislative history, led the court to view this second step as not being a non-discretionary duty of EPA (and instead a discretionary duty with respect to the timing of promulgation)—hence unenforceable by citizen suit. EPA has since identified additional classes of facilities, but has not yet proposed the actual requirements for any of these facilities to demonstrate financial responsibility.[85]

In its report on H.R. 6091, the House Appropriations Committee stated its position that no funding should be provided to develop or implement Superfund financial responsibility requirements, at least until EPA completes an analysis of the capacity of the financial and credit markets to provide the necessary instruments for facilities to demonstrate their financial responsibility.[86] The committee noted its concern that proceeding with new financial responsibility requirements under current economic conditions may impose an undue burden on the affected industries. As a practical matter, some also have questioned whether existing financial responsibility requirements promulgated under other statutes may lessen the need for similar requirements under CERCLA.[87] Still, the adequacy of existing requirements continues to be an issue among those concerned about the capability of facility owners and operators to fulfill their potential liability under CERCLA, if a release of hazardous substances were to occur. Supporters of Superfund financial responsibility requirements contend that the burden of cleanup costs could be shifted to the federal and state taxpayer if responsible parties are incapable of fulfilling their liability.

Special Accounts

Fiscal budgetary constraints also have focused greater attention on EPA's management of private settlement funds obtained from responsible parties, which augment discretionary Superfund appropriations. These private settlement funds are deposited into site-specific Special Accounts within the Superfund Trust Fund. Section 122(b)(3) of CERCLA authorizes EPA to retain these funds and directly use them to finance the cleanup of the sites covered under the settlements, without being subject to discretionary appropriations.[88] Once all planned future work is completed at a site, EPA may "reclassify" the funds remaining in a "Special Account" to pay for work needed at other sites, or may transfer the remaining funds to the general portion of the Superfund Trust Fund to be made available for discretionary appropriations.

In its FY2013 Congressional Justification, EPA reported that it had deposited a total of $3.7 billion in private settlement funds into site-specific Special Accounts over time, and that a total of $1.8 billion remained available for obligation in 992 special accounts as of the end of FY2011.[89]

---

[85] For information on the classes of facilities that EPA has identified and the status of these regulatory developments, see EPA's Superfund program website: http://www.epa.gov/superfund/policy/financialresponsibility.

[86] See H.Rept. 112-589, p. 61-62.

[87] For example, EPA has established financial responsibility requirements under the Resource Conservation and Recovery Act for facilities that store, treat, or dispose of hazardous wastes. The Bureau of Land Management also has established financial responsibility requirements under the Federal Land Policy and Management Act for the reclamation of hardrock mining operations conducted on federal public lands. States also may establish similar financial responsibility requirements under their own laws.

[88] 42 U.S.C. §9622(b)(3).

[89] See EPA's FY2013 Congressional Justification, p. 1046.

Although this remaining balance is greater than the level of annual discretionary Superfund appropriations, Special Account funds are intended to finance all future cleanup work planned at the sites covered under the settlements over the long term. As such, this remaining balance does not represent the level of annual funding available to EPA from Special Accounts. At some sites, Special Account funds may be expended over several years, or even decades in some cases, to complete construction of all cleanup remedies and operate and maintain them over the long term.

In its report on H.R. 6091, the House Appropriations Committee acknowledged the progress that EPA has made in developing centralized procedures to manage Special Account funds more effectively.[90] However, the committee still expressed its concern about the pace at which the $1.8 billion available balance in Special Accounts may be spent in the future. The committee directed EPA to submit a report within 120 days of enactment examining the "practical and legal implications" of reprioritizing Special Account funds currently allocated for long-term future work, and identifying alternative uses of the funds to address near-term risks at other sites.[91]

The use of Special Account funds is governed by the site-specific settlements under which the responsible parties paid the funds to EPA. The authority of EPA to reprioritize and reallocate these funds among other sites would depend on the terms and conditions of the individual settlements. As such, it should be emphasized that Special Account funds are not subject to agency reprogramming authorities in the same manner as discretionary appropriations. Furthermore, if Special Account funds for long-term work were reallocated and spent for other purposes, there could be a need for appropriations in later years to replace the reallocated funds. Otherwise, EPA may not be able to perform that work when needed to ensure the protection of human health and the environment in accordance with CERCLA.

Superfund Alternative Agreements

In its report on H.R. 6091, the House Appropriations Committee expressed interest in EPA's use of Superfund Alternative agreements at some sites, in lieu of EPA listing them on the NPL. Under these agreements, EPA may elect not to pursue the listing of an otherwise eligible site, if the responsible party voluntarily enters into a settlement agreement to perform the cleanup. These agreements are intended to address the cleanup liability of the parties and to free up Superfund appropriations for other sites. The avoidance of an NPL listing may encourage a responsible party to settle if that party is concerned about its association with the site. Some communities also may wish to avoid the perceived stigma of an NPL listing because of possible impacts on property values or economic development.

In its report on H.R. 6091, the House Appropriations Committee directed EPA to continue reporting annually on the use of Superfund Alternative agreements by EPA Region.[92] In its FY2013 Congressional Justification, EPA reported that there were 51 Superfund Alternative agreements covering 67 sites.[93] (The number of agreements is smaller than the number of sites

---

[90] See Government Accountability Office, *Superfund: Status of EPA's Efforts to Improve Its Management and Oversight of Special Accounts*, GAO-12-109, January 2012, available at http://www.gao.gov/products/GAO-12-109.

[91] H.Rept. 112-589, p. 62.

[92] H.Rept. 112-589, p. 62.

[93] See EPA's FY2013 Congressional Justification, p. 679. For a list of each site with a Superfund Alternative agreement in place by EPA Region, see EPA's Superfund program website: http://www.epa.gov/oecaerth/cleanup/superfund/saa-sites.html.

because some agreements cover multiple sites). The number of sites covered under these alternative agreements is a relatively small fraction of the more than 1,600 sites that EPA has listed on the NPL historically, including federal facilities and deleted sites.

If the responsible parties are willing to perform the cleanup, listing a site on the NPL is not essential from a funding standpoint because Superfund appropriations are not needed. As noted earlier, a site must be listed on the NPL to be eligible for Superfund appropriations to pay for the long-term Remedial actions. CERCLA generally authorizes EPA to enter into settlements with responsible parties to allow them to perform the cleanup, and settlements are used at many NPL sites to address cleanup liability. The difference in the use of settlements under the Superfund Alternative approach is that EPA elects not to pursue the listing of the site on the NPL, as long as the responsible party performs the cleanup satisfactorily in accordance with the agreement.

Sites cleaned up under these agreements are not strictly precluded from being listed on the NPL, but EPA's expectation is that listing them will not be necessary to achieve the cleanup. The performance of the cleanup itself is subject to the same process under CERCLA as those that are listed on the NPL. As such, this approach is an alternative to listing a site on the NPL, but is not an alternative to the Superfund cleanup process. EPA asserts that the Superfund Alternative approach has the potential to save the time and resources associated with listing a site on the NPL, contingent upon the responsible parties performing the cleanup satisfactorily.[94] However, some have expressed concern that the lack of an NPL listing may reduce public transparency and awareness of potential hazards at these sites.

Proposed Reinstatement of Superfund Taxes

Interest in greater resources to enhance cleanup progress also has raised the issue of whether the dedicated industry taxes that once helped to finance the Superfund program should be reinstated. Excise taxes on the sale of petroleum and chemical feedstocks, and a special environmental tax on corporate income historically provided the majority of funding for the Superfund Trust Fund. The authority to collect these taxes expired on December 31, 1995. As the remaining revenues were expended over time, Congress has increased the contribution of tax revenues from the General Fund of the U.S. Treasury to the Superfund Trust Fund, in an effort to make up for the shortfall in revenues from the expired industry taxes.[95]

Whether to reinstate Superfund taxes has been a long-standing controversy for over 15 years. The debate has involved numerous issues regarding whether the taxes ensure that polluters pay for the cleanup of contamination, or whether the taxes may place an unfair burden of the costs on certain parties who did not cause or contribute to contamination.[96] Reinstatement of the taxes would be

---

[94] For additional information on the objectives and criteria for the use of Superfund Alternative agreements, see EPA's Superfund program website: http://www.epa.gov/oecaerth/cleanup/superfund/saa.html.

[95] Congress now finances the Superfund Trust Fund mostly with general Treasury revenues, but other sources continue to contribute revenue, including interest on the balance of the trust fund, fines and penalties collected for violations of cleanup requirements, and recovery of cleanup costs from the responsible parties. Although the dedicated industry taxes have expired, industry has continued to contribute revenues that support the Superfund Trust Fund through general Treasury revenues, in the form of corporate income taxes, along with individual income taxes and miscellaneous receipts.

[96] For more information, see the "Hazardous Substance Superfund Trust Fund" section in CRS Report R41039, *Comprehensive Environmental Response, Compensation, and Liability Act: A Summary of Superfund Cleanup Authorities and Related Provisions of the Act*, by David M. Bearden.

subject to the enactment of reauthorizing legislation. The President's FY2013 budget request included a legislative proposal to reinstate Superfund taxes through 2022 and estimated total revenues of nearly $21 billion over that period.[97] At least four bills to reauthorize Superfund taxes have been introduced in the 112th Congress to date: H.R. 1596, H.R. 1634, H.R. 3638 (Subtitle G of Title II), and S. 461.

Brownfields[98]

EPA also administers another cleanup program to provide financial assistance to state, local, and tribal governmental entities for certain types of sites, referred to as "brownfields." Sites eligible for this assistance tend to be sites where the known or suspected presence of contamination may present an impediment to economic development, but where the risks generally are not high enough for the site to be addressed under the Superfund program or other related cleanup authorities. Consistent with liability under CERCLA, responsible parties at these brownfields sites are not eligible for this federal financial assistance, as they are to be held accountable for the cleanup costs. Accordingly, the Brownfields program focuses on providing federal financial assistance for "orphan" sites at which the potential need for cleanup remains unaddressed.[99]

EPA's Brownfields program awards two different categories of grants, one competitive and one formula-based. Section 104(k) of CERCLA authorizes EPA to award competitive grants to state, local, and tribal governmental entities for the assessment and remediation (i.e., cleanup) of eligible brownfields sites, job training for cleanup workers, and technical assistance.[100] Section 128 authorizes EPA to award formula-based grants to help states and tribes enhance their own cleanup programs. These grants are funded within the STAG account, whereas EPA's expenses to administer the Brownfields program are funded within the EPM account.

In reporting H.R. 6091, the House Appropriations Committee recommended a total of $131.2 million within the STAG and EPM accounts combined for EPA's Brownfields program, $35.3 million less than the President's FY2013 request of $166.5 million, and $36.6 million less than the FY2012 enacted appropriation of $167.8 million. The committee's proposed decrease is attributed to a 36% reduction below the President's request for Brownfields competitive grants, and a 37% reduction below the FY2012 enacted appropriation. In proposing this decrease, the committee did note its support for "the continued work of the Brownfields program, but at a reduced rate."[101] The committee also included language within its bill that would prohibit EPA from using more than 25% of the Section 104(k) grant funds to address petroleum sites. Under existing law, Section 104(k) requires that 25% of these funds be set aside for petroleum sites, but does not explicitly prohibit EPA from allocating a higher percentage.

---

[97] OMB, *Budget of the U.S. Government for FY2013*, "Analytical Perspectives," p. 206 and p. 219.

[98] This section was written by David M. Bearden, Specialist in Environmental Policy, CRS Resources, Science, and Industry Division.

[99] For more information on the scope and purpose of this program, see the "Brownfields Properties" section in CRS Report R41039, *Comprehensive Environmental Response, Compensation, and Liability Act: A Summary of Superfund Cleanup Authorities and Related Provisions of the Act*, by David M. Bearden.

[100] Nonprofit organizations also may be eligible for site-specific remediation (i.e., cleanup) grants, subject to a determination by EPA based on certain statutory criteria.

[101] H.Rept. 112-589, p. 65.

Table 6 presents appropriations for EPA's Brownfields program proposed for FY2013 in H.R. 6091, as reported by the House Appropriations Committee, compared to the President's FY2013 request, and appropriations enacted from FY2010 through FY2012. These amounts are presented by EPA account for the competitive and formula grants awarded under the program, and EPA's expenses to administer the program.

Table 6. Appropriations for EPA's Brownfields Program:
FY2010-FY2012 Enacted, and Proposed for FY2013 in the President's Budget
Request and House Committee-Reported H.R. 6091

(millions of dollars)

Account/ Program Area	FY2010 Enacted P.L. 111-88	FY2011 Enacted P.L. 112-10	FY2012 Enacted P.L. 112-74	FY2013 President's Request	FY2013 House Committee H.R. 6091
State and Tribal Assistance Grants					
Section 104(k) Competitive Project Grants[a]	$100.0	$99.8	$94.8	$93.3	$60.0
Section 128 Categorical Grants to States and Tribes[b]	$49.5	$49.4	$49.3	$47.6	$47.6
Brownfields STAG Grant Total	$149.5	$149.2	$144.1	$140.9	$107.6
Environmental Programs and Management					
EPA Administrative Expenses	$23.9	$23.7	$23.6	$25.7	$23.6
Brownfields Program Total	**$173.4**	**$172.9**	**$167.8**	**$166.5**	**$131.2**

Source: Prepared by the Congressional Research Service. FY2010 enacted amounts are as presented in the conference report to accompany the Interior, Environment, and Related Agencies Appropriations Act for FY2010 (H.R. 2996, H.Rept. 111-316, pp. 240–244). FY2011 enacted amounts are the prior-year amounts presented by the House Appropriations Committee in its report accompanying the Interior, Environment, and Related Agencies Appropriations Bill, 2012 (H.R. 2584, H.Rept. 112-151, pp. 192-200). FY2012 enacted amounts, and the FY2013 proposed amounts, are as presented by the House Appropriations Committee in its report accompanying the Interior, Environment, and Related Agencies Appropriations Bill, 2013 (H.R. 6091, H.Rept. 112-589, pp. 170-177). FY2011 and FY2012 enacted amounts reflect applicable rescissions. Numbers may not add due to rounding.

a. Section 104(k) of CERCLA authorizes EPA to award competitive grants to eligible entities for the assessment or remediation (i.e., cleanup) of brownfields to prepare them for redevelopment, job training for cleanup workers, and technical assistance.

b. Section 128 of CERCLA authorizes EPA to award grants to states and tribes on a formula basis to establish or enhance their own cleanup programs.

Leaking Underground Storage Tank (LUST) Program[102]

As indicated in **Table 7** below, House committee-reported H.R. 6091 included $104.1 million for EPA from the Leaking Underground Storage Tank (LUST) Trust Fund, the same as the President's FY2013 request and roughly the same as the FY2012 level, but less than the enacted amounts for the previous two fiscal years. These trust fund monies are used by states and EPA to implement the LUST corrective action and the underground storage tank (UST) leak prevention programs. In addition to the $104.1 million from the trust fund for these activities the House committee-reported bill also included $12.3 million for FY2013 within the EPM account to support EPA staff and extramural expenses used for preventing releases from USTs,[103] the same as the FY2013 request, but slightly less than the FY2012 level. An additional $1.5 million, the same as requested and nearly the same as the previous fiscal year, was included within the STAG account for categorical grants to support state implementation of certain other UST leak prevention and detection regulations that are not eligible for LUST trust fund money.

Congress established the LUST Trust Fund to provide a source of funds for EPA and states to conduct cleanups where no responsible party has been identified, where a responsible party fails to comply with a cleanup order, in the event of an emergency, and to take cost recovery actions against parties. EPA and states have been successful in getting responsible parties to perform most cleanups, and historically, states have used the bulk of their annual LUST Trust Fund grant to oversee and enforce corrective actions performed by UST owners and operators.[104] The trust fund is supported by a 0.1 cent-per-gallon motor fuels tax and had a balance of $3.33 billion as of the beginning of FY2012.[105]

EPA and the states (through cooperative agreements) use appropriated LUST funds primarily to oversee and enforce LUST cleanup activities conducted by responsible parties. Funds also are used to take emergency actions to respond to petroleum releases that may present more immediate risks, clean up abandoned tank sites, and pursue cost recovery actions against the responsible parties.[106]

Since the program began, the frequency and severity of releases from USTs have declined markedly, as regulations intended to prevent and detect releases have been developed and enforced over time and as progress has been made in responding to known releases. Through

---

[102] This section was written by Mary Tiemann, Specialist in Environmental Policy, CRS Resources, Science, and Industry Division. For further discussion, CRS Report RS21201, *Leaking Underground Storage Tanks (USTs): Prevention and Cleanup*, by Mary Tiemann.

[103] EPA is developing regulations to update existing UST requirements and add new requirements for secondary containment and operator training as needed to implement provisions of the Energy Policy Act of 2005. See 76 *Federal Register* 71708, November 18, 2011.

[104] As amended, Subtitle I of the Solid Waste Disposal Act (42 U.S.C. §6991-6991m) authorizes the use of the LUST Trust Fund.

[105] Office of Management and Budget, *Fiscal Year 2013 Budget of the U.S. Government*, Appendix, February 13, 2012, p. 1202, http://www.whitehouse.gov/sites/default/files/omb/budget/fy2013/assets/epa.pdf.

[106] The Senate surface transportation reauthorization bill (S. 1813, MAP-21) would transfer $3.0 billion from the LUST trust fund into the highway trust fund in FY2012, and one-third of future fund receipts. The bill would also extend the LUST trust fund taxing authority through September 30, 2013. See CRS Report R42445, *Surface Transportation Reauthorization Legislation in the 112th Congress: MAP-21, H.R. 7, and H.R. 4348—Major Provisions*, coordinated by Robert S. Kirk.

FY2011, cleanup had been initiated or completed at 82.5% of the roughly 501,000 confirmed release sites, while a backlog of some 88,000 contaminated sites remained.[107]

The Energy Policy Act of 2005 (EPAct 2005, P.L. 109-58) expanded the leak prevention provisions in the UST regulatory program, imposed new responsibilities on the states and EPA, such as requiring states to inspect all tanks every three years. EPAct also broadened the authorized uses of the LUST Trust Fund to support state implementation of the new leak prevention and detection requirements, in addition to supporting the LUST cleanup program. Congress now appropriates funds from the trust fund to support both the LUST cleanup program and the UST leak prevention and detection program. Before EPAct 2005, the UST program had been supported entirely from general revenues. As noted above, a relatively small portion of the total UST program funding is now derived from general revenues.

Program funding has posed a perennial issue. The LUST Trust Fund balance has grown annually as appropriations from the trust fund have remained lower than annual tax receipts and interest earned on the unexpended balance of the fund. Whether or not Congress should increase appropriations from the trust fund to support state leak prevention and cleanup programs has been an issue among the states. States note both the backlog of sites needing remediation and the increased need for resources to comply with the additional UST leak prevention requirements added by EPAct 2005.

Although substantial progress has been made in responding to known releases, an emerging issue is whether the effect of alternative fuels on storage tank infrastructure has caused more leaks and may increase the need for cleanup funds in the future. The renewable fuel mandates in EPAct and the Energy Independence and Security Act of 2007 (EISA; P.L. 110-140) present new technical issues for USTs and for fuel storage, delivery and dispensing infrastructure, generally. EISA requires a substantially increasing use of biofuels each year, and blending ethanol into gasoline is the least-cost and most available option thus far.[108] Most storage tanks are not designed to account for the potential effects of blends of ethanol above 10% by volume (E10) on the structural integrity of the tanks over time. EPA estimates that half of the tanks in the ground are 20 years old and have never been tested for compatibility with higher ethanol blends. Tank owners, EPA, states, and industry are concerned that a new wave of leaks could occur as the amount of ethanol blended in gasoline increases to meet EISA renewable fuel requirements. Under this scenario, EPA expects that more leaks would occur, potentially contaminating groundwater at some sites and possibly placing more demands on state programs and the LUST Trust Fund if the responsible parties are not financially capable of paying for the cleanup. In addition to continuing to implement EPAct requirements, a key area of work for EPA is assessing the compatibility of USTs with alternative fuels and evaluating the transport and degradation characteristics of ethanol and biodiesel blends in groundwater.

---

[107] Environmental Protection Agency, Office of Underground Storage Tanks, *Semiannual Report Of UST Performance Measures End Of Fiscal Year 2011 (October 1, 2010 – September 30, 2011)*, November 2011, available at http://www.epa.gov/OUST/cat/ca_11_34.pdf.

[108] For further discussion of biofuels issues, see CRS Report R40155, *Renewable Fuel Standard (RFS): Overview and Issues*, by Randy Schnepf and Brent D. Yacobucci.

Table 7. Appropriations for the Leaking Underground Storage Tank Trust Fund Program Account: FY2010-FY2012 Enacted, Proposed for FY2013 in the President's Budget Request and House Committee-Reported H.R. 6091

(millions of dollars)

Account/Program Area	FY2010 Enacted P.L. 111-88	FY2011 Enacted P.L. 112-10	FY2012 Enacted P.L. 112-74	FY2013 Requested	FY2013 House Committee H.R. 6091
LUST Account					
EPAct Provisions	$34.4	$34.4	$30.4	$32.4	$32.4
Total LUST Account	$113.1	$112.9	$104.1	$104.1	$104.1
EPM Account					
Underground Storage Tanks (LUST/UST)	$12.5	$13.0	$12.8	$12.3	$12.3
STAG Account					
Categorical Grant: UST	$2.5	$2.5	$1.5	$1.5	$1.5

Source: Prepared by the Congressional Research Service. FY2010 enacted appropriations are as presented in the conference report to accompany the Interior, Environment, and Related Agencies Appropriations Act for FY2010 (H.R. 2996, H.Rept. 111-316, pp. 240–244). The FY2011 and FY2012 enacted amounts and the FY2013 requested amounts are as presented in information provided by the House Appropriations Committee to CRS. FY2012 enacted amounts, FY2013 requested, and House committee-reported bill amounts are as presented in the House Appropriations Committee Report (H.Rept. 112-589) accompanying H.R. 6091 as reported on July 10, 2012. The FY2011 and FY2012 enacted amounts reflect applicable rescissions. Numbers may not add due to rounding.

Geographic-Specific/Ecosystem Programs[109]

The Environmental Programs and Management (EPM) account includes funding for several geographic-specific/ecosystem programs to address certain environmental and human health risks in a number of identified areas of the United States. These programs often involve collaboration among EPA, state and local governments, communities, and nonprofit organizations. **Table 8** presents a comparison of the FY2013 funding included in H.R. 6091 as reported by the House Appropriations Committee with the President's FY2013 request and with FY2010 through FY2012 enacted appropriations for geographic-specific/ecosystem program areas identified as individual line-items in the request.

---

[109] Claudia Copeland, Specialist in Resources and Environmental Policy, CRS Resources, Science, and Industry Division was a primary contributor to this section.

Table 8. Appropriations for Selected Geographic-Specific/Ecosystem Programs: FY2010-FY2012 Enacted, Proposed for FY2013 in the President's Budget Request and House Committee-Reported H.R. 6091

(millions of dollars)

Geographic/Ecosystem Program	FY2010 Enacted P.L. 111-88	FY2011 Enacted P.L. 112-10	FY2012 Enacted P.L. 112-74	FY2013 Requested	FY2013 House Committee H.R. 6091
Water: Ecosystems Total	$58.5	$53.3	$48.2	$55.0	$48.2
National Estuary Program	$32.6	$26.7	$27.0	$27.3	$27.0
Great Lakes Legacy Act[a]	$0.0	$0.0	$0.0	$0.0	$0.0
Wetlands	$25.9	$26.5	$21.2	$27.7	$21.2
Geographic Programs Total	$608.4	$416.0	$409.7	$411.7	$346.3
Great Lakes Restoration Initiative	$475.0	$299.4	$299.5	$300.0	$250.0
Great Lakes Program[a]	$0.0	$0.0	$0.0	$0.0	$0.0
Chesapeake Bay Program	$50.0	$54.4	$57.3	$72.6	$50.0
San Francisco Bay	$7.0	$5.3	$5.8	$4.9	$4.9
South Florida	—	$1.7	$2.1	$1.7	$1.7
Puget Sound	$50.0	$38.1	$30.0	$19.3	$30.0
Long Island Sound Program	$7.0	$5.3	$4.0	$3.0	$3.0
Gulf of Mexico Program	$6.0	$4.6	$5.5	$4.4	$4.4
Lake Champlain Basin Program	$4.0	$3.0	$2.4	$1.4	$1.4
Lake Pontchartrain	$1.5	$1.1	$2.0	$1.0	$1.0
Community Action for Renewed Environment (CARE)	$2.4	$1.9	$0.0	$2.1	$0.0
Other Geographic Programs and Regional Initiatives	$5.5	$1.2	$1.3	$1.4	$0.0
Total Ecosystem/Geographic Programs	**$666.9**	**$469.3**	**$457.9**	**$466.7**	**$394.5**

Source: Prepared by the Congressional Research Service. FY2010 enacted appropriations are as presented in the conference report to accompany the Interior, Environment, and Related Agencies Appropriations Act for FY2010 (H.R. 2996, H.Rept. 111-316, pp. 240–244). The FY2011 and FY2012 enacted amounts and the FY2013 requested amounts are as presented in information provided by the House Appropriations Committee to CRS. FY2012 enacted amounts, FY2013 requested and House committee-reported bill amounts are as presented in the House Appropriations Committee Report (H.Rept. 112-589) accompanying H.R. 6091 as reported on July 10, 2012. The FY2011 and FY2012 enacted amounts reflect applicable rescissions. Numbers may not add due to rounding.

a. Funding for the Great Lakes Legacy Act and for EPA's Great Lakes Program was moved to the Great Lakes Restoration Initiative in FY2010.

Great Lakes Restoration Initiative

In 2004, President Bush established a Great Lakes Interagency Task Force, chaired by EPA,[110] to develop a strategy (released in 2005) that will guide federal Great Lakes protection and restoration efforts. To better coordinate these efforts, the FY2010 budget requested, and Congress endorsed in P.L. 111-88, a Great Lakes Restoration Initiative involving EPA and eight other federal agencies. The purpose of the initiative is to target the most significant problems in the ecosystem, such as aquatic invasive species, nonpoint source pollution, and toxics and contaminated sediment.[111] Projects and programs are to be implemented through grants and agreements with states, tribes, municipalities, universities, and other organizations. The initiative consolidates funding for a number of existing federal Great Lakes programs, including EPA's Great Lakes National Program Office (GLNPO), its implementation of the Great Lakes Legacy Act to clean up contaminated sediments, and other agencies' Great Lakes programs.

The $250.0 million[112] recommended for FY2013 for the Great Lakes Restoration Initiative within the EPM account by the House committee is $50.0 million less than requested for FY2013 and $49.5 million less than the FY2012 enacted level, and $175.0 million below the FY2010 enacted appropriations of $475.0 million. Some Members and stakeholders have expressed concern about the reduced funding level since FY2011.

Chesapeake Bay

In May 2009, President Obama issued *Executive Order 13508: Chesapeake Bay Protection and Restoration*, which directed federal departments and agencies to exercise greater leadership in implementing their existing authorities to restore the Bay. Despite restoration efforts of the past 25 years, which have resulted in some successes in specific parts of the ecosystem, the overall health of the Bay remains degraded by excessive levels of nutrients and sediment. As indicated in **Table 8**, for FY2013 the House committee recommended $50.0 million to implement its Chesapeake Bay program, the same level as enacted for FY2010 but $22.6 million less than the FY2013 President's budget request, $7.3 million less than FY2012, and $4.4 million less than FY2011. Of the funding proposed by the House committee for FY2013, $8.0 million is for nutrient management and sediment removal grants, and $2.0 million is for small watershed grants to control polluted runoff from urban, suburban, and agricultural lands.[113] The FY2013 President's requested increase for the program was intended to accelerate pollution reduction and aquatic habitat restoration efforts in the Bay, consistent with the objectives of the 2009 executive order.

---

[110] The Great Lakes Interagency Task Force was established by Executive Order in 2004; for information see http://www.epa.gov/glnpo/iatf/index.html.

[111] For information, see the Great Lakes Restoration Initiative website, http://greatlakesrestoration.us/.

[112] An Administrative Provision under Title II of the FY2013 House committee-reported bill (H.R. 6091) would authorize the EPA Administrator to transfer up to $250.0 million of the funds appropriated for the Great Lakes Restoration Initiative (GLRI) within the EPM account to other federal departments or agencies to carry out projects supporting the GLRI and the Great Lakes Water Agreement programs, projects, or activities.

[113] H.Rept. 112-589, p. 52.

National (Congressional) Priorities and Earmarks

The House Appropriations Committee specified a combined total of $20.0 million for "National Priorities" within the Science and Technology (S&T) and the Environmental Programs and Management (EPM) accounts for FY2013, roughly the same combined total included in the FY2012 enacted appropriations.[114] The $5.0 million specified under the S&T account for FY2013 in the House committee report (H.Rept. 112-589) for "Research: National Priorities" is slightly higher than the amount included for FY2012 after accounting for rescissions. The funding is to be used for competitive extramural research grants to fund high-priority water quality and availability research by not-for-profit organizations who often partner with the agency.[115] Additionally, $15.0 million was specified for FY2013 for "Environmental Protection: National Priorities" in the EPM account to be used for competitive grants for qualified nonprofits to provide rural and urban communities with technical assistance to improve water quality and provide safe drinking water. Of the total, which again is slightly higher than FY2012 after accounting for rescissions, $13.0 million would be for providing training and technical assistance on a national level, or multi-state regional basis, and $2.0 million would be for providing technical assistance to private drinking water well owners.[116]

The House committee has adhered to an earmark moratorium during the 112th Congress as put forth by the leadership in both chambers, generally precluding earmarks in the appropriations bills for FY2011, FY2012, and FY2013.[117] The moratorium followed the adoption of definitions of earmarks in House and Senate rules. While there is no consensus on a single earmark definition among all practitioners and observers of the appropriations process, the Senate and House both in 2007 adopted separate definitions for purposes of implementing new earmark transparency requirements in their respective chambers.[118] In the House rule, such a funding item is referred to as a *congressional earmark* (or *earmark*), while, in the Senate rule, it is referred to as a *congressionally directed spending item* (or *spending item*).[119]

---

[114] See H.Rept. 112-331 accompanying P.L. 112-74.

[115] H.Rept. 112-589, p. 47.

[116] Ibid., p. 51.

[117] *Rules of the House Republican Conference for the 112th Congress, Standing Orders*, December 8, 2010, p. 43, http://www.gop.gov/about/rules?standing-orders-for-the-112th; Senate Committee on Appropriations, *Committee Announces Earmark Moratorium*, February 1, 2011 Press Release, http://appropriations.senate.gov/news.cfm?method=news.view&id=188dc791-4b0d-459e-b8d9-4ede5ca299e7.

[118] See Senate Rule XLIV and House Rule XXI, clause 9. CRS Report RL34462, *House and Senate Procedural Rules Concerning Earmark Disclosure*, by Sandy Streeter, describes and compares the procedures and requirements in House and Senate rules. See also CRS Report RS22866, *Earmark Disclosure Rules in the House: Member and Committee Requirements*, by Megan Suzanne Lynch, and CRS Report RS22867, *Earmark Disclosure Rules in the Senate: Member and Committee Requirements*, by Megan Suzanne Lynch.

[119] In both cases, this refers to "a provision [in a measure or conference report] or report language included primarily at the request of a [Representative or] Senator providing, authorizing, or recommending a specific amount of discretionary budget authority, credit authority, or other spending authority for a contract, loan, loan guarantee, grant, loan authority, or other expenditure with or to an entity, or targeted to a specific state, locality or Congressional district, other than through a statutory or administrative formula-driven or competitive award process." Senate Rule XLIV and House Rule XXI, clause 9.

Appendix A. Historical Funding Trends and Staffing Levels

The Nixon Administration established EPA in 1970 in response to growing public concern about environmental pollution, consolidating federal pollution control responsibilities that had been divided among several federal agencies. Congress has enacted an increasing number of environmental laws, as well as major amendments to these statutes, over three decades following EPA's creation.[120] Annual appropriations provide the funds necessary for EPA to carry out its responsibilities under these laws, such as the regulation of air and water quality, use of pesticides and toxic substances, management and disposal of solid and hazardous wastes, and cleanup of environmental contamination. EPA also awards grants to assist state, tribal, and local governments in controlling pollution in order to comply with federal environmental requirements, and to help fund the implementation and enforcement of federal regulations delegated to the states.

Table 1 presents FY2008-FY2012 enacted appropriations and the President's FY2013 budget request for EPA by each of the eight accounts.

Figure A-1 presents a history of total discretionary budget authority for EPA from FY1976 through FY2012, and the President's FY2013 budget request, as reported by the Office of Management and Budget (OMB) in the "Historical Tables" accompanying the President's *Budget of the U.S. Government, Fiscal Year 2013*. Levels of agency budget authority prior to FY1976 were not reported by OMB in the Historical Tables. In **Figure A-1**, the levels of discretionary budget authority are presented in nominal dollars as reported by OMB, and are adjusted for inflation by CRS to reflect the trend in real dollar values over time. EPA's historical funding trends generally reflects the evolution of the agency's responsibilities over time, as Congress has enacted legislation to authorize the agency's programs and activities in response to a range of environmental issues and concerns. In terms of the overall federal budget, EPA's annual appropriations have represented a relatively small portion of the total discretionary federal budget (just under 1% in recent years).

Without adjusting for inflation, EPA's funding has grown from $1.0 billion when EPA was established in FY1970 to a peak funding level of $14.86 billion in FY2009. This peak includes regular fiscal year appropriations of $7.64 billion provided for FY2009 in P.L. 111-8 and the emergency supplemental appropriations of $7.22 billion provided for FY2009 in P.L. 111-5. However, in real dollar values (adjusted for inflation), EPA's funding in FY1978 was slighter more than the level in FY2009, as presented in **Figure A-1**.

---

[120] For a discussion of these laws, see CRS Report RL30798, *Environmental Laws: Summaries of Major Statutes Administered by the Environmental Protection Agency*.

Table A-1. Appropriations for the Environmental Protection Agency: FY2008-FY2012 Enacted, and Proposed for FY2013 in the President's Budget Request and House Committee-Reported H.R. 6091

(millions of dollars not adjusted for inflation)

	FY2008 P.L. 110-161	FY2009 Omnibus P.L. 111-8	FY2009 ARRA P.L. 111-5	FY2009 Total	FY2010 P.L. 111-88	FY2011 P.L. 112-10	FY2012 P.L. 112-74	FY2013 Requested	FY2013 House Comm. H.R. 6091
Science and Technology									
—Base Appropriations	$760.1	$790.1	$0.0	$790.1	$848.1a	$813.5	$793.7	$807.3	$734.8
—Transfer in from Superfund	+$25.7	+$26.4	$0.0	+$26.4	+$26.8	+$26.8	+$23.0	+$23.2	+$23.0
Science and Technology Total	$785.8	$816.5	$0.0	$816.5	$874.9	$840.3	$816.7	$830.5	$761.3
Environmental Programs and Management	$2,328.0	$2,392.1	$0.0	$2,392.1	$2,993.8	$2,756.5	$2,678.2	$2,817.2	$2,479.1
Office of Inspector General									
—Base Appropriations	$41.1	$44.8	$20.0	$64.8	$44.8	$44.7	$41.9	$48.3	$41.9
—Transfer in from Superfund	+$11.5	+$10.0	$0.0	+$10.0	+$10.0	+$10.0	+$9.9	+$10.9	+$9.9
Office of Inspector General Total	$52.6	$54.8	$20.0	$74.8	$54.8	$54.7	$51.8	$59.1	$51.9
Buildings & Facilities	$34.3	$35.0	$0.0	$35.0	$37.0	$36.4	$36.4	$42.0	$36.4
Hazardous Substance Superfund (before transfers)	$1,254.0	$1,285.0	$600.0	$1,885.0	$1,306.5	$1,280.9	$1,213.8	$1,176.4	$1,164.9
—Transfer out to Office of Inspector General	-$11.5	-$10.0	$0.0	-$10.0	-$10.0	-$10.0	-$9.9	-$10.9	-$9.9
—Transfer out to Science and Technology	-$25.7	-$26.4	$0.0	-$26.4	-$26.8	-$26.8	-$23.0	-$23.2	-$23.0
Hazardous Substance Superfund (after transfers)	$1,216.8	$1,248.6	$600.0	$1,848.6	$1,269.7	$1,244.2	$1,180.9	$1,142.3	$1,132.0
Leaking Underground Storage Tank Trust Fund Program	$105.8	$112.6	$200.0	$312.6	$113.1	$112.9	$104.1	$104.1	$104.1
Inland Oil Spill Program (formerly Oil Spill Response)	$17.1	$17.7	$0.0	$17.7	$18.4	$18.3	$18.2	$23.5	$18.2

Environmental Protection Agency (EPA): Appropriations for FY2013

	FY2008 P.L. 110-161	FY2009 Omnibus P.L. 111-8	FY2009 ARRA P.L. 111-5	FY2009 Total	FY2010 P.L. 111-88	FY2011 P.L. 112-10	FY2012 P.L. 112-74	FY2013 Requested	FY2013 House Comm. H.R. 6091
State and Tribal Assistance Grants (STAG)									
—Clean Water State Revolving Fund	$689.1	$689.1	$4,000.0	$4,689.1	$2,100.0	$1,522.0	$1,466.5	$1,175.0	$689.0
—Drinking Water State Revolving Fund	$829.0	$829.0	$2,000.0	$2,829.0	$1,387.0	$963.1	$917.9	$850.0	$829.0
—Special (Congressional) Project Grants	$132.9	$145.0	$0.0	$145.0	$156.8	$0.0	$0.0	$0.0	$0.0
—Categorical Grants	$1,078.3	$1,094.9	$0.0	$1,094.9	$1,116.4	$1,104.2	$1,088.8	$1,202.4	$994.0
—Brownfields Section 104(k) Grants	$93.5	$97.0	$100.0	$197.0	$100.0	$99.8	$94.8	$93.3	$60.0
—Diesel Emission Reduction Grants	$49.2	$60.0	$300.0	$360.0	$60.0	$49.9	$30.0	$15.0	$30.0
—Other State and Tribal Assistance Grants	$54.2	$53.5	$0.0	$53.5	$50.0	$19.9	$15.0	$20.9	$0.0
State and Tribal Assistance Grants Total	$2,926.2	$2,968.5	$6,400.0	$9,368.5	$4,970.2	$3,758.9	$3,612.9	$3,355.7	$2,602.0
Rescissions of Unobligated Balances[b]	-$5.0	-$10.0	$0.0	-$10.0	-$40.0	-$140.0	-$50.0	-$30.0	-$130.0
Total EPA Accounts	**$7,461.5**	**$7,635.7**	**$7,220.0**	**$14,855.7**	**$10,291.9[a]**	**$8,682.1**	**$8,449.4**	**$8,344.5**	**$7,055.0**

Source: Prepared by CRS using the most recent information available from House, Senate, or conference committee reports accompanying the annual appropriations bills that fund EPA and Administration budget documents, including the President's annual budget requests as presented by OMB, and EPA's accompanying annual congressional budget justifications. "ARRA" refers to the American Recovery and Reinvestment Act of 2009 (P.L. 111-5). The ARRA amounts do not reflect rescission of unobligated balances as per P.L. 111-226. Numbers may not add due to rounding.

a. The amounts presented for the base appropriations for the S&T account and the EPA total include $2.0 million in supplemental appropriations for research of the potential long-term human health and environmental risks and impacts from the releases of crude oil, and the application of chemical dispersants and other mitigation measures under P.L. 111-212, Title II.

b. The FY2008-FY2010 rescissions are from unobligated balances from funds appropriated in prior years within the eight accounts, and made available for expenditure in a later year. In effect, these "rescissions" increase the availability of funds for expenditure by the agency in the years in which they are applied, functioning as an offset to new appropriations by Congress. With regard to the FY2011 enacted rescissions, Sec. 1740 in Title VII of Div. B under P.L. 112-10 refers only to "unobligated balances available for 'Environmental Protection Agency, State and Tribal Assistance Grants'" [not across all accounts], and does not specify that these funds are to be rescinded from prior years. For FY2012 enacted, under the Administrative Provisions in Division E, Title II of P.L. 112-74, unobligated balances from the STAG ($45.0 million) and the Hazardous Substance Superfund ($5.0 million) accounts would be rescinded. FY2012 rescissions specified within the STAG account include $20.0 million from categorical grants, $10.0 million from the Clean Water SRF, and $5.0 million each from Brownfields grants, Diesel Emission Reduction Act grants, and Mexico Border. The rescission included for FY2013 in H.R. 6091 and the President's FY2013 request would be from prior years' unobligated balances within the STAG account.

**Figure A-1. EPA Discretionary Budget Authority FY1976-FY2012 and
FY2013 President's Request: Adjusted and Not Adjusted for Inflation**

($ in billions)

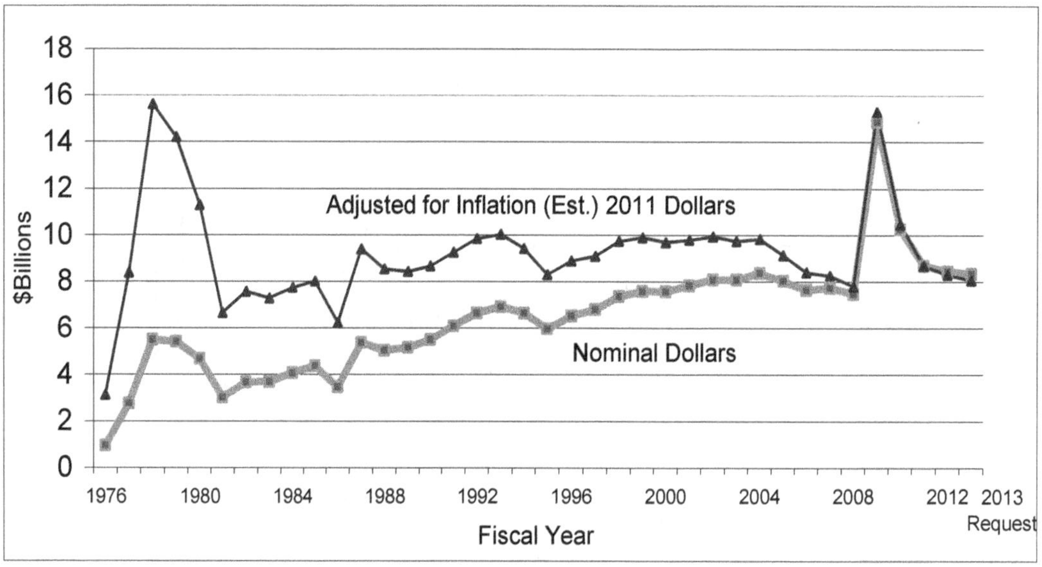

Source: Prepared by CRS with information from the Office of Management and Budget, *Budget of the United States Government Fiscal Year 2013, Historical Table:* Table 5-4. CRS converted nominal dollars to 2011 dollars using the GDP Chained Price Index from Table 10.1 *Gross Domestic Product and Deflators Used in the Historical Tables - 1940–2017,* http://www.whitehouse.gov/omb/budget/Historicals.

Note: FY1976 was the earliest fiscal year for which historical funding information on budget authority was readily available from the Office of Management and Budget.

EPA Staff Levels

In its report (H.Rept. 112-589) accompanying H.R. 6091 as reported, the House committee expressed concerns about the distribution of EPA regional "Full Time Equivalents"[121] (FTEs) to headquarters, and directed the agency to bring the headquarters FTE level in line with the regional levels. EPA is also directed by the committee to cap its total FTEs at no more than 16,594, the FY2010 level, similar to direction provided in the FY2012 Interior, Environment, and Related Agencies conference report. The committee believes EPA can achieve this reduction of 515 FTEs below the FY2013 budget request with the funding provided.[122]

Figure A-2 below provides a trend in EPA's authorized FTE employment ceiling from FY2001 through FY2013, the last year of which is based on the levels proposed by the House committee and the President's request. Information prior to FY2001 is available in a March 2000 testimony by the Government Accountability Office (GAO),[123] in which GAO reported that EPA FTEs

---

[121] As noted in **Figure A-2**, FTE employment is defined as one employee working full time for a full year (52 weeks X 40 hours = 2,080 hours), or the equivalent hours worked by several part-time or temporary employees.

[122] H.Rept. 112-589, p. 57.

[123] Government Accounting Office (GAO), March 23, 2000, Testimony Before the Subcommittee on VA, HUD, and Independent Agencies, Senate Committee on Appropriations, *Human Capital: Observations on EPA's Efforts to* (continued...)

---

increased by about 18% from FY1990 through FY1999, with the largest increase (13%, from 15,277 to 17,280 FTEs) occurring from FY1990 though FY1993. From FY1993 through FY1999, GAO indicated that EPA's FTEs grew at a more moderate rate at less than 1% per year. As indicated in **Figure A-2**, with the exception of increases in four fiscal years, there has been a general downward trend since FY2001, with the largest single-year decrease (2.3%) occurring from FY2011 to FY2012.

Figure A-2. EPA's Authorized Full Time Equivalent (FTE) Employment Ceiling, FY2001-FY2012 Actual and FY2013 Requested and Proposed

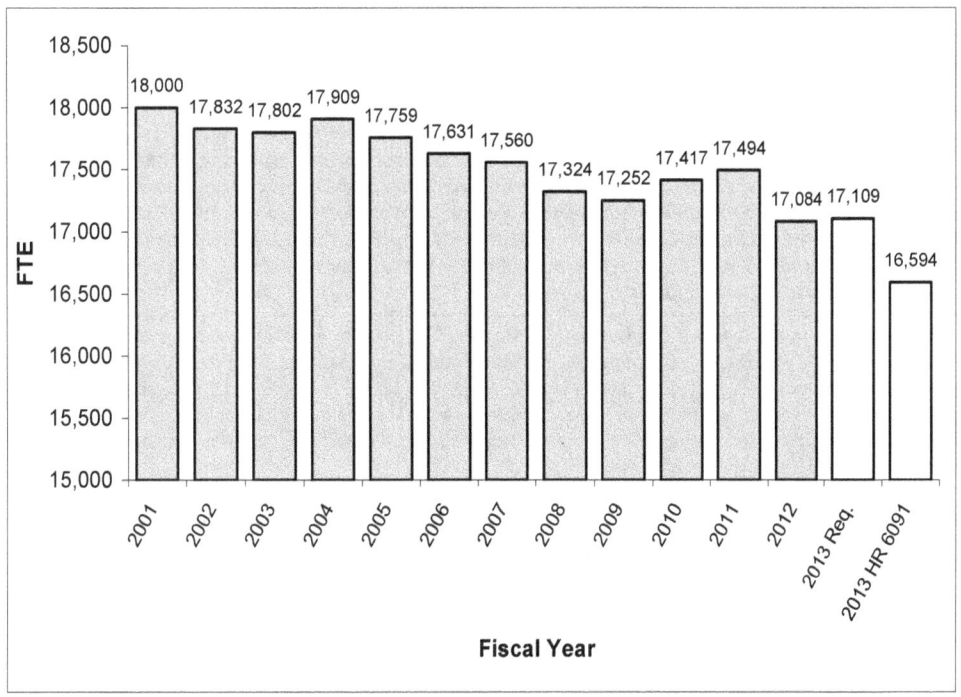

Source: Prepared by the Congressional Research Service as adapted from EPA's "FY2013 EPA Budget in Brief"; see "Overview" p. 12 (pdf p. 15), http://www.epa.gov/planandbudget/annualplan/fy2013.html#FY13budget, and H.Rept. 112-589, p. 57.

Notes: Full Time Equivalent or FTE is defined as one employee working full time for a full year (52 weeks X 40 hours = 2,080 hours), or the equivalent hours worked by several part-time or temporary employees. FY2013 FTEs are as proposed in the President's FY2013 budget request.

(...continued)

Implement a Workforce Planning Strategy, Statement for the Record by Peter F. Guerrero, Director, Environmental Protection Issues, Resources, Community, and Economic Development Division, GAO/T-RCED-00-129, http://www.spa.ga.gov/word/wfpArticles/GAO%20EPA.pdf.

Appendix B. Descriptions of EPA's Eight Appropriations Accounts

Since FY1996, EPA's funding has been requested by the Administration and appropriated by Congress under eight statutory accounts. **Table B-1** describes the scope of the programs and activities funded within each of these accounts. Prior to FY1996, Congress appropriated funding for EPA under a different account structure, making it difficult to compare funding for the agency historically over time by the individual accounts.

Table B-1. EPA's Eight Appropriations Accounts

Science and Technology (S&T): The S&T account incorporates elements of the former Research and Development account that was in place until FY1996. The S&T account funds the development of the scientific knowledge and tools necessary to inform EPA's formulation of pollution control regulations, standards, and agency guidance. EPA carries out research activities not only at its own laboratories and facilities, but also through contracts, grants, and cooperative agreements with other federal agencies, state and local governments, nonprofit organizations, universities, and private businesses. Congress appropriates funds directly to the S&T account and transfers additional funds from the Hazardous Substances Superfund account to the S&T account specifically to support research related to the cleanup of hazardous substances.

Environmental Programs and Management (EPM): The EPM account funds a broad range of activities involved in EPA's development of pollution control regulations and standards, and enforcement of these requirements across multiple environmental media, such as air quality and water quality. The EPM account also funds technical assistance to pollution control agencies and organizations, and technical assistance on how regulated entities can assure compliance with environmental requirements to avoid violations. Much of EPA's administrative and operational expenses are funded within this account as well.

Office of Inspector General (OIG): As amended, the Inspector General Act of 1978 established Offices of Inspector General in numerous federal agencies, including EPA. These offices are intended to conduct independent auditing, evaluation, and investigation of an agency's programs and activities to identify potential management and administrative deficiencies, which may create conditions for instances of fraud, waste, and mismanagement of funds, and to recommend actions to correct these deficiencies. Congress appropriates funds directly to EPA's OIG account and transfers additional funds from the Hazardous Substances Superfund account to the OIG account specifically to support the office's auditing, evaluation, and investigation of the Superfund program.

Buildings and Facilities: This account funds the construction, repair, improvement, extension, alteration, and purchase of fixed equipment and facilities owned or used by EPA.

Hazardous Substance Superfund: This account is funded by discretionary appropriations from a dedicated trust fund of the same name, the Hazardous Substance Superfund Trust Fund. As amended, the Comprehensive Environmental Response, Compensation, and Liability Act of 1980 (CERCLA) established the Superfund program to clean up the nation's most threatening sites and created the Superfund Trust Fund to finance the program. Dedicated taxes on industry originally provided most of the revenues to the Superfund Trust Fund, but the taxing authority expired at the end of 1995. Congress now finances this trust fund mostly with revenues from the General Fund of the U.S. Treasury. EPA may use appropriations from the Superfund Trust Fund to enforce the liability of "potentially responsible parties" for the cleanup of contaminated sites, and if the parties cannot be found or cannot pay at a site, EPA may pay for the cleanup under a cost-share agreement with the state in which the site is located. Although the Superfund account also funds EPA's oversight of the cleanup of federal facilities by other agencies, these agencies fund the actual cleanup with separate funds appropriated directly to them, not with Superfund monies.

Inland Oil Spill Program (formerly Oil Spill Response): As authorized by the Oil Pollution Act of 1990, this account funds EPA's activities to prepare for and prevent releases of oil into the inland zone of the United States within the agency's jurisdiction. The U.S. Coast Guard has jurisdiction over oil spills in the coastal zone of the United States. EPA is reimbursed for its expenses to respond to oil spills at inland sites from the Oil Spill Liability Trust Fund, which is administered by the U.S. Coast Guard. The former name of the "Oil Spill Response" account was changed by the conferees as proposed in the President's FY2012 request to "Inland Oil Spill Program." This modification was intended to more clearly reflect the agency's jurisdiction for oil spill response in the inland coastal zone.

The Leaking Underground Storage Tank (LUST) Trust Fund Program: Like the Superfund account, this account is funded by discretionary appropriations from a dedicated trust fund of the same name, the LUST Trust Fund. The Superfund Amendments and Reauthorization Act of 1986 established this trust fund. The LUST Trust Fund is financed primarily by a 0.1 cent per gallon tax on motor fuels, authorized through FY2016. EPA may use appropriations from the LUST Trust Fund to pay for the prevention of, and response to, releases from underground storage tanks that contain petroleum, which is not covered under Superfund. EPA and the states (through cooperative agreements) may use the funds to oversee corrective actions (i.e., cleanup) performed by the responsible parties, to conduct cleanups where a responsible party fails to do so or in case of an emergency, and to recover LUST monies spent on cleanup from the responsible parties. In addition to these activities, the Energy Policy Act of 2005 expanded the authorized uses of appropriated LUST monies to include implementation and enforcement of EPA's Underground Storage Tank leak prevention and detection program.

State and Tribal Assistance Grants (STAG): The majority of the funding within the STAG account is for capitalization grants for the Clean Water and Drinking Water State Revolving Funds (SRFs). SRF funding is used for local wastewater and drinking water infrastructure projects, such as construction of and modifications to municipal sewage treatment plants and drinking water treatment plants, to facilitate compliance with Clean Water Act and Safe Drinking Water Act requirements, respectively. The remainder of the STAG account funds other water infrastructure grants, categorical grants to states and tribes for numerous pollution control activities, grants for the cleanup of brownfields, and diesel emission reduction grants. Although the majority of funding for grants awarded by EPA is funded within the STAG account, other agency accounts also fund various types of grants, such as the S&T and EPM accounts.

Appendix C. Selected Provisions Contained in House Committee-Reported H.R. 6091 and Accompanying Report

House committee-reported H.R. 6091 included several provisions and report language within most of EPA's appropriations accounts and a number of administrative provisions at the end of Title II, setting terms and conditions for certain EPA activities. The relatively more controversial provisions regarding several EPA programs and regulations were contained in the "General Provisions" in Title IV of H.R. 6091. **Table C-1** through **Table C-6**, which follow, identify those provisions in the House committee-reported bill. The provisions included in H.R. 6091 presented in the following tables are categorized in this report by general program areas, that is, air quality and climate change, water quality, and waste management. Related provisions that are under the jurisdiction of agencies other than EPA are listed separately in **Table C-6**. The tables contain information about the provisions, including the associated sections of the bill and those that were amendments adopted during full-committee markup, if applicable.

Several of the general provisions included in House committee-reported H.R. 6091 for FY2013 are the same or similar to several provisions included in the enacted FY2012 appropriations (P.L. 112-74),[124] and a subset of those proposed for FY2012 in H.R. 2584 as reported by the House Appropriations Committee on July 19, 2011,[125] and for FY2011 in the Full-Year Continuing Appropriations Act, 2011 (H.R. 1), as passed by the House on February 19, 2011.[126] These provisions were not included in the final FY2011 appropriations law (P.L. 112-10) enacted April 15, 2011.

---

[124] See CRS Report R42332, *Environmental Protection Agency (EPA) FY2012 Appropriations*, by Robert Esworthy.

[125] See CRS Report R41979, *Environmental Protection Agency (EPA) FY2012 Appropriations: Overview of Provisions in H.R. 2584 as Reported*, by Robert Esworthy

[126] See CRS Report R41698, *H.R. 1 Full-Year FY2011 Continuing Resolution: Overview of Environmental Protection Agency (EPA) Provisions*, by Robert Esworthy.

Table C-1. EPA Air Quality, Climate Change, and Greenhouse Gas Emissions Program Activities General Provisions

EPA Activity/Program Description	Air Quality/Climate Change/Greenhouse Gas Emissions Provisions in House Committee-Reported H.R. 6091		
	Section	Bill Text	House Action
Climate change reporting use of funds (all federal departments and agencies)	Sec. 419. Title IV REPORT ON CLIMATE CHANGE FUNDS	"Not later than 120 days after the date on which the President's fiscal year 2014 budget request is submitted to Congress, the President shall submit a comprehensive report to the Committee on Appropriations of the House of Representatives and the Committee on Appropriations of the Senate describing in detail all Federal agency funding, domestic and international, for climate change programs, projects and activities in fiscal year 2012, including an accounting of funding by agency with each agency identifying climate change programs, projects and activities and associated costs by line item as presented in the President's Budget Appendix, and including citations and linkages where practicable to each strategic plan that is driving funding within each climate change program, project and activity listed in the report."	Included in FY2013 draft appropriations bill as approved by House Interior, Environmental and Related Agencies Appropriations Subcommittee
Title V of the Clean Air Act (42 U.S.C. 7661 et seq.): livestock production	Sec. 420. Title IV PROHIBITION ON USE OF FUNDS	"Notwithstanding any other provision of law, none of the funds made available in this Act or any other Act may be used to promulgate or implement any regulation requiring the issuance of permits under title V of the Clean Air Act (42 U.S.C. 7661 et seq.) for carbon dioxide, nitrous oxide, water vapor, or methane emissions resulting from biological processes associated with livestock production."	Included in FY2013 draft appropriations bill as approved by House Interior, Environmental and Related Agencies Appropriations Subcommittee
Greenhouse gas emissions: manure mgt.	Sec. 421. Title IV GREENHOUSE GAS REPORTING RESTRICTIONS	"Notwithstanding any other provision of law, none of the funds made available in this or any other Act may be used to implement any provision in a rule, if that provision requires mandatory reporting of greenhouse gas emissions from manure management systems."	Included in FY2013 draft appropriations bill as approved by House Interior, Environmental and Related Agencies Appropriations Subcommittee

EPA Activity/Program Description	Air Quality/Climate Change/Greenhouse Gas Emissions Provisions in House Committee-Reported H.R. 6091		
	Section	Bill Text	House Action
48-month pilot project for the North American Emission Control Area	Sec. 440. Title IV EMISSION CONTROL ACT PILOT	"(a) The Administrator of the Environmental Protection Agency, in consultation with the Commandant of the Coast Guard, shall carry out a 48-month pilot project for the North American Emission Control Area under which— (1) subject to paragraph (2), the owner or operator of a vessel opting into the pilot project is deemed to be in compliance with United States sulfur content fuel requirements if— (A) the vessel meets requirements under the International Convention for the Prevention of Pollution from Ships, 1973/78 (MARPOL), Annex VI, Regulation 4; and (B) the Administrator determines that compliance with the requirements described in subparagraph (A) provides a degree of overall protection of the public health and welfare (based on fleet averaging, weighted averaging, weighted and unweighted emissions averaging calculations, and such other measures as determined appropriate by the Administrator) that is equivalent to the degree of such protection provided by compliance with United States sulfur content fuel requirements; and (2) the owner or operator of a vessel opting into the pilot project continues to be subject to United States sulfur content fuel requirements while at berth or anchor. (b) For purposes of evaluating the results of such pilot project, the Administrator of the Environmental Protection Agency shall complete atmospheric modeling and actual ambient air testing to determine the environmental and economic effectiveness of United States sulfur content fuel requirements, in combination with the requirements described in subsection (a)(1)(A), particularly as such effectiveness relates to Alaska and Hawaii. (c) In this section: (1) The term "North American Emission Control Area" means the North American Emission Control Area designated pursuant to the Act to Prevent Pollution from Ships. (2) The term "United States sulfur fuel requirements" means the requirements under Federal and State law applicable to the sulfur content of the fuel used for operation of the vessel."	Adopted as an amendment during full-committee markup June 27-28, 2012
Greenhouse gas emissions: mobile source emissions Sections 202 and 209(b) of the Clean Air Act (42 U.S.C. 7521 and 42 U.S.C. 7543(b))	Sec. 444. Title IV MOBILE SOURCE EMISSION	"None of the funds made available under this Act shall be used- (1) to prepare, propose, promulgate, finalize, implement, or enforce any regulation pursuant to section 202 of the Clean Air Act (42 U.S.C. 7521) regarding the regulation of any greenhouse gas emissions from new motor vehicles or new motor vehicle engines that are manufactured after model year 2016 to address climate change; or (2) to consider or grant a waiver under section 209(b) of such Act (42 U.S.C. 7543(b)) so that a State or political subdivision	Adopted as an amendment during full-committee markup June 27-28, 2012

EPA Activity/Program Description	Air Quality/Climate Change/Greenhouse Gas Emissions Provisions in House Committee-Reported H.R. 6091		
	Section	Bill Text	House Action
		thereof may adopt or attempt to enforce standards for the control of emissions of any greenhouse gas from new motor vehicles or new motor vehicle engines that are manufactured after model year 2016 to address climate change."	
Asbestos National Emission Standards for Hazardous Air Pollutants (NESHAPS) regulations (subpart M of part 61 of title 40, Code of Federal Regulations)	Sec. 446. Title IV ASBESTOS NESHAP	"None of the funds made available by this Act may be used to implement, administer, or enforce the National Emission Standards for Hazardous Air Pollutants regulations for asbestos under subpart M of part 61 of title 40, Code of Federal Regulations with respect to any residential building that has 4 or fewer dwelling units, unless such building falls within the definition of "installation" under such regulations."	Adopted as an amendment during full-committee markup June 27-28, 2012
Greenhouse gas emissions: Prohibit New Source Performance Standards (NSPS) under section 111 of the CAA	Sec. 448. Title IV GHG NSPS	"None of the funds made available by this Act may be used to develop, issue, implement, or enforce any regulation or guidance under section 111 of the Clean Air Act establishing any standard of performance applicable to the emission of any greenhouse gas by any new or existing source that is an electric utility generating unit."	Adopted as an amendment during full-committee markup June 27-28, 2012
EPA Air Pollution Control Cost Manual seventh edition update	Sec. 449. Title IV COST MANUAL UPDATE	"Not later than 30 days after the date of enactment of this Act, the Administrator of the Environmental Protection Agency shall begin development of a seventh edition of the document entitled "EPA Air Pollution Control Cost Manual". The Administrator shall consult, and seek comment from, State, local, and tribal departments of environmental quality during development of such seventh edition, and provide opportunity for public comment."	Adopted as an amendment during full-committee markup June 27-28, 2012
Solicit guidance on air quality models (appendix W to part 51 of title 40, Code of Federal Regulations)	Sec. 450. Title IV COMMENTS ON AIR QUALITY MODELS	"Not later than 30 days after the date of enactment of this Act, the Administrator of the Environmental Protection Agency shall publish in the Federal Register a notice to solicit comment on revising the Agency's "Guideline on Air Quality Models" under appendix W to part 51 of title 40, Code of Federal Regulations, to allow flexible modeling approaches and to adopt the most recently published version of the CALPUFF modeling system (or portions thereof) as a preferred air quality model under such Guideline."	Adopted as an amendment during full-committee markup June 27-28, 2012

Source: Prepared by CRS based on provisions as contained in H.R. 6091, Interior, Environment, and Related Agencies Subcommittee FY2013 appropriations bill as reported by the House Appropriations Committee on July 10, 2012, and adopted amendments as reported by the House Appropriations Committee following the June 27-June 28, 2012, full-committee markup of the subcommittee draft bill, http://appropriations.house.gov/uploadedfiles/fy13interioradopted.pdf.

Table C-2. EPA Water Quality Program Activities Provisions

EPA Activity/Program Description	Water Quality Program Activities Provisions Included in House Committee-Reported H.R. 6091		
	Section	Bill Text	House Action
Sec. 402(l) of the Federal Water Pollution Control Act (33 U.S.C. 1342(l))	Sec. 422. Title IV SILVICULTURAL ACTIVITIES	"Section 402(l) of the Federal Water Pollution Control Act (33 U.S.C. 1342(l)) is amended by adding at the end the following: '(3) SILVICULTURAL ACTIVITIES- The Administrator shall not require a permit under this section, nor shall the Administrator directly or indirectly require any State to require a permit, for discharges of stormwater runoff from roads, the construction, use, or maintenance of which are associated with silvicultural activities, or from other silvicultural activities involving nursery operations, site preparation, reforestation and subsequent cultural treatment, thinning, prescribed burning, pest and fire control, harvesting operations, or surface drainage.' "	Included in FY2013 draft appropriations bill as approved by House Interior, Environmental and Related Agencies Appropriations Subcommittee
Definition of waters under the jurisdiction of the Federal Water Pollution Control Act (33 U.S.C. 1251 et seq.) (See Sec. for FY2012	Sec. 434. Title IV WATERS OF THE UNITED STATES	"None of the funds made available by this Act or any subsequent Act making appropriations for the Environmental Protection Agency may be used by the Environmental Protection Agency to develop, adopt, implement, administer, or enforce a change or supplement to the rule dated November 13, 1986, as amended August 25, 1993, or guidance documents dated January 15, 2003, and December 2, 2008, pertaining to the definition of waters under the jurisdiction of the Federal Water Pollution Control Act (33 U.S.C. 1251 et seq.)."	Included in FY2013 draft appropriations bill as approved by House Interior, Environmental and Related Agencies Appropriations Subcommittee

EPA Activity/Program Description	Water Quality Program Activities Provisions Included in House Committee-Reported H.R. 6091		
	Section	**Bill Text**	**House Action**
Sec. 402(p) of the Federal Water Pollution Control Act (33 U.S.C. 1342(p))	Sec. 436. Title IV STORMWATER DISCHARGE	"None of the funds made available by this Act or any other Act may be expended for the development, adoption, implementation, or enforcement of regulations or guidance that would expand the Federal stormwater discharge program under section 402(p) of the Federal Water Pollution Control Act (33 U.S.C. 1342(p)) to post-construction commercial or residential properties until 90 days after the Administrator of the Environmental Protection Agency submits to the Committee on Transportation and Infrastructure and the Committee on Appropriations of the House of Representatives and the Committee on Environment and Public Works and the Committee on Appropriations of the Senate the study of stormwater discharges required under section 402(p)(5) of such Act (33 U.S.C. 1342(p)(5)). Such study shall include— (1) a thorough review and analysis of potential regulatory options under the stormwater program; (2) the program's anticipated costs (including to the Environmental Protection Agency, States, and potentially regulated entities) and benefits; and (3) a numerical identification of both relative cost effectiveness among the options and the anticipated water quality enhancements that would result from each option."	Included in FY2013 draft appropriations bill as approved by House Interior, Environmental and Related Agencies Appropriations Subcommittee
Sect. 402(p)(3) of the Federal Water Pollution Control Act (33 U.S.C. 1342(p)(3))	Sec. 441. Title IV MUNICIPAL SEPARATE STORM SEWER SYSTEM PERMITTING	Section 402(p)(3) of the Federal Water Pollution Control Act (33 U.S.C. 1342(p)(3)) is amended by adding at the end the following new subparagraph: " '(C) LIMITATION.—The Administrator or a State may not require a municipality operating a municipal separate storm sewer system serving a population of less than 100,000 to obtain a permit under this subsection for a discharge that— "(i) is composed entirely of stormwater from a facility that is not owned or operated by the municipality; and "(ii) does not enter into the municipal separate storm sewer system.' "	One of several amendments adopted as part of the Manager's Amendment during full-committee markup June 27-28, 2012

EPA Activity/Program Description	Water Quality Program Activities Provisions Included in House Committee-Reported H.R. 6091		
	Section	Bill Text	House Action
Require U.S. iron and steel products for construction projects under Title VI of the Federal Water Pollution Control Act (33 U.S.C. 1381 et seq.) and section 1452 of the Safe Drinking Water Act (42 U.S.C. 300j–12).	Sec 442. Title IV BUY AMERICAN	(a)(1) None of the funds made available by a State water pollution control revolving fund as authorized by title VI of the Federal Water Pollution Control Act (33 U.S.C. 1381 et seq.) or made available by a drinking water treatment revolving loan fund as authorized by section 1452 of the Safe Drinking Water Act (42 U.S.C. 300j–12) shall be used for a project for the construction, alteration, maintenance, or repair of a public water system or treatment works unless all of the iron and steel products used in the project are produced in the United States. (2) In this section, the term "iron and steel products" means the following products made primarily of iron or steel: lined or unlined pipes and fittings, manhole covers and other municipal castings, hydrants, tanks, flanges, pipe clamps and restraints, valves, structural steel, reinforced precast concrete, and construction and building materials. (b) Subsection (a) shall not apply in any case or category of cases in which the Administrator of the Environmental Protection Agency (in this section referred to as the "Administrator") finds that— (1) applying subsection (a) would be inconsistent with the public interest; (2) iron and steel products are not produced in the United States in sufficient and reasonably available quantities and of a satisfactory quality; or (3) inclusion of iron and steel products produced in the United States will increase the cost of the overall project by more than 25 percent. (c) If the Administrator receives a request for a waiver under this section, the Administrator shall provide an informal notice of and opportunity for public comment on the request at least 15 days before making a finding based on the request. Notice provided under this subsection shall include the information available to the Administrator concerning the request and shall be provided by electronic means, including on the official public Internet Web site of the Environmental Protection Agency. (d) This section shall be applied in a manner consistent with United States obligations under international agreements. (e) The Administrator may retain up to 1 percent of the funds appropriated by this Act for carrying out the provisions described in subsection (a)(1) for management and oversight of the requirements of this section. (f) This section does not apply with respect to a project if a State agency approves the engineering plans and specifications for the project, in that agency's capacity to approve such plans and specifications prior to a project requesting bids, prior to October 1, 2012, or the date of the enactment of this Act, whichever is later.	Adopted as an amendment during full-committee markup June 27-28, 2012

Source: Prepared by CRS based on provisions as contained in H.R. 6091, Interior, Environment, and Related Agencies Subcommittee FY2013 appropriations bill as reported by the House Appropriations Committee on July 10, 2012, and adopted amendments as reported by the House Appropriations Committee following the June 27-June 28, 2012, full-committee markup of the subcommittee draft bill, http://appropriations.house.gov/uploadedfiles/fy13interioradopted.pdf.

Table C-3. EPA Superfund Program Provisions

EPA Activity/Program Description	EPA Superfund Program: Provisions Included in House Committee-Reported H.R. 6091		
	Section	Bill Text	House Action
Superfund cleanup financial responsibility requirements under Section 108(b) of the Comprehensive Environmental Response, Compensation, and Liability Act (CERCLA)of 1980 (42 U.S.C. 9608(b))	Sec. 447. Title IV FINANCIAL ASSURANCE	"None of the funds made available by this Act may be used to develop, propose, finalize, implement, enforce, or administer any regulation that would establish new financial responsibility requirements pursuant to section 108(b) of the Comprehensive Environmental Response, Compensation, and Liability Act of 1980 (42 U.S.C. 9608(b))."	Adopted as an amendment during full-committee markup June 27-28, 2012

Source: Prepared by CRS based on provisions as contained in H.R. 6091, Interior, Environment, and Related Agencies Subcommittee FY2013 appropriations bill as reported by the House Appropriations Committee on July 10, 2012, and adopted amendments as reported by the House Appropriations Committee following the June 27-June 28, 2012, full-committee markup of the subcommittee draft bill, http://appropriations.house.gov/uploadedfiles/fy13interioradopted.pdf.

Table C-4. EPA Toxic Chemical Regulatory Programs

EPA Activity/Program Description	Toxic Chemical Regulatory Programs Provisions Included in House Committee-Reported H.R. 2584		
	Section	Bill Text	House Action
Lead Renovation, Repair, and Painting Rule (subpart E of part 745 of title 40, Code of Federal Regulations)	Sec. 443. Title IV LEAD TEST KIT	"None of the funds made available by this Act may be used to implement or enforce regulations under subpart E of part 745 of title 40, Code of Federal Regulations (commonly known as the 'Lead; Renovation, Repair, and Painting Rule'), or any subsequent amendments to such regulations, until the Administrator of the Environmental Protection Agency publicizes Environmental Protection Agency recognition of a commercially available lead test kit that meets both criteria under section 745.88(c) of title 40, Code of Federal Regulations."	Adopted as an amendment during full-committee markup June 27-28, 2012

Source: Prepared by CRS based on provisions as contained in H.R. 6091, Interior, Environment, and Related Agencies Subcommittee FY2013 appropriations bill as reported by the House Appropriations Committee on July 10, 2012, and adopted amendments as reported by the House Appropriations Committee following the June 27-June 28, 2012, full-committee markup of the subcommittee draft bill, http://appropriations.house.gov/uploadedfiles/fy13interioradopted.pdf.

Table C-5. EPA Pesticide Programs Provisions

EPA Activity/Program Description	Pesticide Programs: Provisions Included in House Committee-Reported H.R. 6091		
	Section	Bill Text	House Action
Pesticide Label requirements under FIFRA	Sec. 445. Title IV PESTICIDE LABELS	"None of the funds made available by this Act may be used by the Administrator of the Environmental Protection Agency to finalize the Proposed Guidance on False or Misleading Pesticide Product Brand Names, as contained in Draft Pesticide Registration Notice 2010–X (Docket ID EPA–HQ–OPP–2010–0282)."	Adopted as an amendment during full-committee markup June 27-28, 2012

Source: Prepared by CRS based on provisions as contained in H.R. 6091, Interior, Environment, and Related Agencies Subcommittee FY2013 appropriations bill as reported by the House Appropriations Committee on July 10, 2012, and adopted amendments as reported by the House Appropriations Committee following the June 27-June 28, 2012, full-committee markup of the subcommittee draft bill, http://appropriations.house.gov/uploadedfiles/fy13interioradopted.pdf.

Table C-6. Related Provisions Not Under EPA's Jurisdiction

EPA Activity/Program Description	Related Provisions Not Under EPA's Jurisdiction Included in House Committee-Reported H.R. 6091		
	Section	Bill Text	House Action
Office of Mining Reclamation and Enforcement, Dept. of the Interior stream buffer zone (Not EPA) (See Sec.	Sec. 435. Title IV STREAM BUFFERS	"None of the funds made available by this Act may be used to develop, carry out, implement, or otherwise enforce proposed regulations published June 18, 2010 (75 Fed. Reg. 34,667) by the Office of Surface Mining Reclamation and Enforcement of the Department of the Interior."	Included in FY2013 draft appropriations bill as approved by House Interior, Environmental and Related Agencies Appropriations Subcommittee

Source: Prepared by CRS based on provisions as contained in H.R. 6091, Interior, Environment, and Related Agencies Subcommittee FY2013 appropriations bill as reported by the House Appropriations Committee on July 10, 2012, and adopted amendments as reported by the House Appropriations Committee following the June 27-June 28, 2012, full-committee markup of the subcommittee draft bill, http://appropriations.house.gov/uploadedfiles/fy13interioradopted.pdf.

Author Contact Information

Robert Esworthy, Coordinator
Specialist in Environmental Policy
resworthy@crs.loc.gov, 7-7236

David M. Bearden
Specialist in Environmental Policy
dbearden@crs.loc.gov, 7-2390

Mary Tiemann
Specialist in Environmental Policy
mtiemann@crs.loc.gov, 7-5937

Claudia Copeland
Specialist in Resources and Environmental Policy
ccopeland@crs.loc.gov, 7-7227

James E. McCarthy
Specialist in Environmental Policy
jmccarthy@crs.loc.gov, 7-7225

Jane A. Leggett
Specialist in Energy and Environmental Policy
jaleggett@crs.loc.gov, 7-9525